THE WONDER OF DIVINE HEALING

THE WONDER
OF DIVINE HEALING

✠

A DIVINE HEALING SYMPOSIUM

✠

Edited by
THE REV. DR. A. A. JONES

✠

Published by
ARTHUR JAMES
The Drift, Evesham, Worcs.

First Edition 1958

© —1958—Arthur James Ltd.

MADE AND PRINTED IN GREAT BRITAIN BY PURNELL AND SONS, LTD.
PAULTON (SOMERSET) AND LONDON

Foreword

by THE BISHOP OF LICHFIELD

I WAS very pleased to be invited by the editor to write a short foreword to this symposium which he is producing, and which I think ought to be of the greatest interest to all those people who are prepared to give careful thought to this important matter of Divine Healing.

The editor has been kind enough to extend this invitation to me in view of the fact that I have the privilege of being the Chairman of the Churches' Council of Healing. This is a federating and supporting Council to the various guilds and individuals who are engaged in the work of Spiritual Healing. As most of them approach this activity from very different viewpoints, it is desirable that there should be an outside body like the Council which can view the work they do purely objectively and help to save the movement from being too closely associated with any particular denominational or sectarian interest. There are different ministries and gifts, but one Spirit. It is this for which the Council stands, and, as such, it has secured the trust of the British Medical Association, a very necessary and important achievement which gives confidence to many who still have a critical attitude to the whole movement.

There is no doubt that the general interest in Spiritual Healing is very much on the increase, and what we are anxious to do is to see that people have correct information and do not misjudge it by reason of false conceptions which they may have had about the work. It is my hope that this symposium will greatly help forward this important activity of enabling the right approach to the work to be widely known, and I therefore have much pleasure in commending this book.

Bishop's House,
Lichfield, 1958.

SHELTON LICHFIELD.

Introduction

THE WONDER OF DIVINE HEALING

by the Editor, THE REV. DR. A. A. JONES

*The Rev. A. A. Jones, M.A., B.D., Ph.D., originally
intended to follow a commercial career but gave this up in
order to study philosophy and theology for four years at Birmingham University, followed by one year at Oxford. For some years
he was Divinity master in a grammar school for boys, and after
ordination in the Church of England became Chaplain and
Lecturer in Divinity at St. Gabriel's College. He is now Vicar
of St. Silas Church, Nunhead, in South-East London.*

IT IS INDEED a wonderful world in which we live, for
it is full of the wonders of divine power which we can see
around us and within us, in God's works of creation and
restoration. So many of these are taken for granted; we rarely
give thought to them. Those who live in sprawling cities or
industrial towns are often too preoccupied to notice the wonder
of spring when the soft new shoots mark out their straight
green lines in gardens and fields, or of the autumn when the
mellow fruits, the golden flowers and leaves offer themselves
for our nourishment or enjoyment.

This same creative and re-creative power of God is at work
within ourselves. A child falls and hurts himself; he runs to
Mother, who kisses the place to make it better, and he takes it
for granted that it will be so. The adult cuts his finger and
puts a plaster on it to help it to heal, and quite naturally

assumes that it will heal. The healing comes through the power of God within us, re-creating or restoring that which is good and which He created in the first instance.

Here is the *first* of the foundations on which our belief in Divine Healing is built. In the beginning God, and in the beginning God created. No capricious deity is this, whose emotions can be aroused, twisted and turned to benevolent interest or bitter hatred by the sacrificial bribes or by the follies of his devotees. The God in whom we trust is the perfect, redeeming, loving Creator revealed to us as Father by His Son Jesus Christ. We believe, on the evidence of Scripture and of the experience of the Church, that His perfect will, which was expressed in His first creative act, has been and always is unchanging and unswerving for man's good. The Psalmist said, "I will remember Thy wonders of old" (Ps. 77: 11); and the aim of this Symposium is to recall us to a proper sense of wonder as we think about the gracious manner in which the power of God works towards our healing.

A devout lady whom I know had to consult a surgeon and was naturally upset when he told her that she would have to undergo a very serious operation, and even then he could not hold out more than a fifty-fifty chance of success. I pointed out to her that that was his honest medical opinion based only on physical considerations, and that he could not introduce into his diagnosis those spiritual factors we know to be vital. If the patient had no religious faith, or was suddenly in this time of crisis brought face to face with neglected religious duties, anxiety and fear would probably make the result of the operation hang in the balance, with the danger of collapse. But my friend was a woman of firm faith and prayer and a regular communicant, and I suggested to her that she should think of Jesus going with her into the operating theatre, and the prayers of our intercessors upholding her at the time of the operation.

A few days later she was sitting up in bed smiling happily, and told me that on the morning after the operation the anæsthetist came to see her and said, "Well, he saw you through all right." She thought he meant the surgeon, but he explained that just before giving the anæsthetic he had told her not to worry but to relax, and she had replied, "I know I shall be all right. He will see me through." She explained to the anæsthetist that she had been thinking of Jesus and trusting in His love and in the power of prayer. Much sooner than the surgeon believed possible, even in his most optimistic moments, she was out of hospital, and today joins with those intercessors who upheld her before the Throne of God.

Not all men, not even all Christians, have acknowledged that the power of God is directed towards our healing, but our Lord Jesus Christ revealed the all-powerful Creator as our Father, and taught that He is a God of Love. The Bible says God *is* Love (1 John 4: 16), and we know that love must always be active or it sinks into mere sentimentality. The love of God is not a static gift to be accepted or rejected, but a vital power by which to live, as the same passage points out: "he that abideth in love abideth in God and God abideth in him." So, as our first reason for rejoicing in the wonder of Divine Healing, we put forward our belief that God created man as the expression of His love, and that He re-creates and restores him as the object of His love.

We reinforce this with our *second* fundamental belief: that God is ever present with us, and ever good. We do not always realise this or think about it, but when we are quiet we echo the words of the Psalmist, "Whither shall I go from thy Spirit? or whither shall I flee from thy presence?" (Ps. 139: 7). God is in the heights and the depths; He is near and He is far; He is in our conscience and He is in the judgement passed on us by the conscience of our generation.

The busy activities of life all too often drive far from our minds all thoughts of God, and our prayers follow the words of General Astley before the Battle of Edgehill in 1642: "O Lord, thou knowest how busy we must be this day. If we forget Thee, do not Thou forget us, for Christ's sake, Amen." We should all be helped if we remembered the words of the lovely ancient Collect which declares that God *is* Light and Life and Strength: "O Thou who art the Light of the minds that know Thee, the Life of the souls that love Thee, and the Strength of the thoughts that seek Thee; help us so to know Thee that we may truly love Thee, so to love Thee that we may fully serve Thee, whose service is perfect freedom; through Jesus Christ our Lord, Amen."

One day, when visiting a friend's house, I found his wife huddled in a blanket in front of a big fire, yet still shivering. I said she ought to go to bed and send for the doctor, but being a busy mother she did not think she could spare the time. Then she added, "In any case, I thought you believed in prayer." I assured her that that was true, but that I also believed in the exercise of common sense and proper precautions. The next day she was not only in bed but in an oxygen tent in hospital struggling for breath. There she found time and quiet to remember her own prayers and to know that her friends in the Church were sending waves of strength as they held her before God in prayers for her healing. Her recovery was so rapid that the doctor said, "We cannot understand how you have got so well so soon." A simple faith does not demand understanding but is content to accept the wonder of Divine Healing.

God is ever with us, restoring our strength when our resistance ceases in sleep, and willing to give us full sufficiency of body, soul and spirit if we turn to Him and allow His life to enter our life. We do not need to go to special places or persons to find Him, but naturally some are better than others, and in committing to the Church the Ministry of Divine Healing, the Lord invites us to meet Him in His own house through the ministry of His own appointed servants.

Our *third* fundamental belief is that God has so made us that our physical body can be made strong through the strengthening of our soul and spirit by the indwelling Spirit of God. St. Paul put it this way: "The Spirit Himself beareth witness with our spirit that we are children of God" (Rom. 8: 16). Our bodies are like musical instruments which respond to the skill and mood of the player. If our minds are strong and our spirits in tune with our Creator, our bodies respond and we are enabled to offer vigorous and willing service.

Sometimes we are depressed and lacking in faith, and although the creative power of God is waiting to flood through us we block the way and our bodies flag. We are discouraged and seem to sink ever deeper in the mire of unbelief though we long to believe, and our footsteps grow feebler though we long to stride out and shake off the prevailing pessimism and cynicism of our generation.

This is where the Church can help. Jesus, having come from His heavenly Father and knowing Him to be our Creator, ever-loving and redeeming, gave instructions to His disciples to go out and take this news to a bewildered world—wonderful news of the healing of the nations and of the heart of man—glorious news of the wonder of God coming to heal and save. When He sent disciples on a short mission tour they were instructed to preach to the text, "The Kingdom of Heaven is at hand", and they were given "authority over unclean spirits, to cast them out, and to heal all manner of disease and all manner of sickness" (Matt. 10: 1). They rejoiced on their return to be able to report the triumphant results of the use of this authority.

In our Lord's final commission to His Church immediately prior to His ascension He commanded them, "Go ye into all the world, and preach the Gospel to the whole Creation", and promised that if this was done "these signs shall follow them that believe: in my name they shall cast out devils: they shall speak with new tongues . . . they shall lay hands on the sick and they shall recover" (Mark 16: 15–18).

Here is a clear enough commission to the Church to preach the Gospel in all its power, thus enlightening the ignorant and encouraging the downcast, and bringing that healing of body and soul which we often call Wholeness. Unfortunately, this is where our problems and difficulties seem to begin. The

Church preaches the Gospel, but how many people listen? Is the Church not certain enough in its utterance, or do we live in unusually evil times? Certainly there is evil enough in the world, and our Lord said that following the faithful preaching devils would be cast out. But in these sophisticated times many people profess not to believe in devils or a devil, but prefer to speak of neuroses, complexes and phobias. The promise that healing power would come if the disciples and their followers laid hands on the sick is being taken very seriously in many parts of the Church today, but still most people who send for the doctor when they are ill quite forget to send for the minister. Indeed, there is some truth in the story of the invalid who was greatly distressed when his wife told him that she had asked the vicar to call, and said to her, "I know I am not well, but surely I am not so ill as all that."

It might seem that at the heart of these problems is an antagonism or antipathy towards the Church, but there are many signs that this is not the case. It would seem rather that, living in a materialistic and scientific age, many people are very sceptical as to whether non-material forces such as faith, prayer, spiritual guidance, can have any effect on material objects such as human bodies. Much fascinating research is being done to find out how far, if at all, the human mind can control or affect inanimate objects. No doubt this has a bearing on the effect of mental states on bodily welfare, but the purpose of these essays is to testify to our belief in the power of a simple faith in Jesus Christ, with the prayer, devotion and fellowship that go with it, to bring healing, health and wholeness to suffering mankind.

Many churches have Prayer Groups which meet regularly, not only to intercede for the sick but to hold them in the fellowship of love in the presence of our Heavenly Father, and as a result of such devotion one often hears the word *Miracle* on the lips of those who only see a wonderful physical recovery. A baby was taken into hospital for an emergency operation, but the surgeon held out no hope, and a priest was summoned to baptise the baby. The priest felt moved not only to baptise but to give the laying on of hands, for he felt certain that the Lord would use the recovery of the child to some wonderful purpose. Afterwards he spoke to the parents and found that the father had become a heavy drinker and was fast losing control of himself and sinking into alcoholism. That simple service and the sight of the babe lying helpless and apparently at death's door did something to that man that no exhortations or good advice had done. Together they knelt and asked for the guidance of God, and the priest took the needs of that family to the loving prayers of his Intercession Group. The baby recovered and the nurses said it was a miracle; true, it was, and more than one miracle, for today, some years after the event, the father proudly takes the lad to church to sing the praises of the God who healed them both.

A small boy was in hospital for months with a serious internal disease, and most people shook their heads sadly and said it was quite hopeless. His mother was a woman of prayer, and though the flame of life in the lad sometimes seemed little more than a spark, her faith never wavered, and she was upheld by the prayers of the Intercession Group at the church. Then came the evening when the doctors said that there was no more they could do. It was also the evening of the prayer meeting, and in perfect faith and love the boy and his mother and the hospital staff were upheld before the God of Love. The next morning there was definite improvement, and within two days he was asking for something to eat. "It's a miracle," whispered one of the nurses. Yes! Although the cynic may not understand, it is the continuing miracle of the mercy of God to sinful, suffering humanity, the tender care of a loving Father towards His children.

We believe that man is a child of God, and is therefore to be considered as more than a body—more even than a mixture of body, soul and spirit. He is a unity, as the Godhead is a unity, and the strengthening of the soul and spirit must have its effect in the strengthening of the body.

This is the theme of the first part of the book, entitled *The Problem*: How can the Ministry of the Church help to make sick men well? Here we have the essays of two medical practitioners, DR. BURNETT RAE and DR. LAMBOURNE; and two clergy, THE BISHOP OF ROCHESTER and the VERY REV. H. C. ROBINS, dealing with some of the difficulties that cross our minds as we consider the existence of illness, amongst other evils, in a world created and ordered by a God of Love.

THE BISHOP OF ROCHESTER shows how the Church has faced the challenge of sickness and evil from the time of the disciples and the early Church Fathers to the present day. He does not minimise the antagonisms that have arisen between Church and Medicine, nor the difficulties raised by the scientific temper of this age, but, writing with the authority of one of the leaders of the Church, he shows that there is now a growing desire to understand all aspects of the Ministry of Divine Healing.

DR. BURNETT RAE writes with the authority of his office as Vice-Chairman of the Churches' Council of Healing, and an extensive clinical experience. He sees health not as a static condition, but as an achievement which is reached when the spirit of man co-operates with the Creator Spirit. The Churches' Council of Healing unites Church and Medicine, and symbolises the unity between the spiritual and the material which makes for health. Dr. Rae believes that we cannot revive Spiritual Healing as it was in the early days of the Church because we cannot ignore the evidence of science, but healing comes when we surrender ourselves to God and use all the knowledge that He has made available, whether spiritual or scientific.

The VERY REV. H. C. ROBINS deals with some of the vital problems that trouble those who are ill or have to look after invalids. He answers the question "Is Disease God's will or is it sent by Him?" with a very firm No, and goes on to deal with the problem of the influence of the Spirit on the mind and the body, and the value of prayer in the healing of sickness.

DR. LAMBOURNE writes as a doctor with a practice in an industrial city where the population lives at close quarters. Families on council estates and men and women in factories are massed together in great communities where rejoicings or misfortunes are apt to be writ large. If one firm fails, hundreds of families suffer, and if two or three children are struck down with polio the chill hand of fear grips the hearts of many parents. In such circumstances the doctor sees and assesses his patients' problems and sufferings against a wide back-cloth of anxious faces and troubled hearts, and he knows that his medical skill needs to be supported by a healing community or fellowship in which his patients can find security. Here is one of the great challenges to the Church today—vast communities standing in desperate need of the Gospel, not preached in orthodox methods but taken by the members of the congregation into the life of their own street or block of flats.

So we turn, in the second part of the book, to *The Answer*, which various writers set out from their own experiences, to the Problem of the Church and Healing, and the Needs of a Sick Society. We start with a moving testimony from HUGH RED-WOOD, who tells how he experienced the wonder of Divine Healing. Struck down by a deadly disease and advised to undergo an operation which, even if successful, would have left him unable to work, he committed himself entirely to the Lord. The prayer of faith and the act of dedication were followed by spiritual renewal and physical healing, and Hugh Redwood has been granted new power in preaching the Gospel and a wonderful message of healing to preach.

CANON DUCKER is one of a small band of clergy who are qualified to offer psychological guidance, and he tells of some of the people he has helped in his pastoral work and the cries of need that he has been able to answer. He regards the needs of ordinary men and women as a great evangelistic opportunity before the Church—the Ministry of Healing and the preaching of the Gospel both flow from the compassion of Christ and His Church.

DR. F. E. ENGLAND stresses the belief that all healing is spiritual and that although doctors and clergy appear to work in different fields it is of the utmost importance that they should seek out every opportunity for co-operation. He maintains that the ultimate aim of the Church's Ministry of Healing is more than bodily fitness and is to be regarded as the patient's adjustment to his ultimate environment or, more simply, personal peace with God.

One of the leaders in the work of bringing doctors and clergy together has been MISS GRAHAM IKIN, and she tells how discussions between them in local meetings or hospital seminars have helped many patients. Particularly is this true when discussions have continued in prayer, and she stresses the need for a prayer group in every church, for prayer opens up new dimensions. Effective intercession releases compassion, and through men of prayer God performs what are sometimes called Miracles of Faith and Miracles of Healing.

It is faith and prayer that bring tranquillity of mind, which is the secret longing of many puzzled people. DR. TORRIE has found that the four main aims pursued by men in search of tranquillity are Material Needs, Security, Fellowship, and Creativeness. The reason why so many fail in their search is that they regard bodily healing or peace of mind as ends in themselves. To be whole in spirit is to be at one with God, and this involves the cutting out of self; perfect trust brings peace of mind, and this leads to the full harmonious working of body, mind and spirit.

This leads to the timely and reassuring message of the REV. WILFRID BOURNE, that Divine Healing is not dependent on gifted "healers". We must believe in God alone as our Healer, and, in complete surrender, trust Him as the source of all wholeness and healing. The use of affirmative prayer has helped many sufferers by directing their intercessions more towards the perfection of God as He is and less towards the activity of God as we would like Him to exercise it on our behalf.

Our last essay is by the REV. DR. MICHAEL WILSON who is

singularly qualified to sum up our human problems and needs, and to underline the divine answer to the sufferings of humanity, for he is highly qualified as a medical practitioner, and has been ordained as a priest in the Church of England. He has worked overseas as a doctor, and in England as a priest, and is thus able to direct those who suffer to the way of Wholeness found in Jesus Christ our Lord.

It is with faith in the healing power of Jesus Christ that this book is offered by the various contributors. We believe that God has put many skills into the hands of men, and expects that we shall use them to the full in the healing ministry, and that He has also put faith into our hearts so that we may allow the healing to be complete, and the sufferer to become a new man in Christ, finding that perfect Wholeness which is the wonder of Divine Healing.

Contents

CONTENTS

✠

PART I

THE PROBLEM

✠

1

THE CHURCH AND DIVINE HEALING

by The Rt. Rev. C. M. Chavasse, Bishop of Rochester

After a distinguished career as an undergraduate at Oxford,
Dr. Chavasse, M.A., D.D., was ordained, served several
curacies, and became Rector of St. Aldate's, Oxford, in 1922.
In 1928 he became the Master of St. Peter's Hall, Oxford,
where he remained until 1939, when he was consecrated as Bishop
of Rochester. He is regarded as a leading spokesman of the
Evangelical School in the Church of England, and is the editor
of Towards the Conversion of England *and the author of*
several books on the Church.

IN ORDER to understand the true value of Divine Healing
and, still more, to practise its effective ministry, there
are certain popular misconceptions as to its nature and
claims which it is necessary to dispel. If, therefore, at first I
seem to pull down, it is in order to build up on a sound and
scriptural foundation.

Its Comprehensive Character

First and foremost, all healing is Divine Healing; not simply
healing in which medical science has no share. God works
through "M. & B." or penicillin just as much as through the
laying on of hands or holy unction. The whole principle of
the Incarnation—that is, of God operative in and through His
world—cries out against the heresy that God is most present
where human endeavour is most absent; or that creative and

redemptive processes which He has ordained become less divine when we know how they work.

Thus Archbishop William Temple in his *Readings in St. John's Gospel* has an illuminating comment on our Lord's promise that His Church should even excel His own mighty works when He had returned to the Father (John 14: 12). "It is a greater thing," wrote Dr. Temple, "to have founded hospitals all over Europe and in many parts of Asia and Africa, than to have healed some scores, or some hundreds, of sick folk in Palestine; and it is to the spirit of Christ at work in the hearts of men that we owe the establishment of hospitals."

CHRIST'S COMPREHENSIVE CHARGE

Thus, in the second place, our Lord's charge "to heal the sick" was general in character and to the whole Church. He did not transmit to the ordained ministry a power, or authority, to heal which rendered medical healing unnecessary. Undoubtedly the Church of the first centuries believed that He had done so. It entered the pagan world as a professedly healing mission, and challenged the cult of Aesculapius at the height of its popularity. It is, therefore, sometimes assumed, and even stated as an accepted fact, that miraculous healing (such as the Gospels and the Acts record) persisted for the first three centuries of the Christian era and then gradually faded out owing to reduced intensity of faith. Thereafter, as we know, from the fifth century onwards there was a general recourse, not to Christian healers, but to the relics of saints in cathedrals and churches, which derived immense revenues thereby.

But an examination of contemporary records gives no ground for such an assumption. The golden age of Greek scientific healing, associated with the name of Hippocrates (born *c.* 460 B.C.), had suffered lamentable decline, and Rome by the beginning of the Christian era was full of quacks, charlatans, poisoners and magicians. The pagan world thus presented an empty field for those possessed of charismatic "gifts of

24

healing" listed by St. Paul at the end of 1 Corinthians 12. Yet long before the end of the third century Justin Martyr, Irenaeus, Tertullian and Origen—born in that order between A.D. 100 and 185—already look back wistfully to the miracles of apostolic times.

The inevitable conclusion is that there were no more miraculous healings effected by the Church in the sub-Apostolic age than we observe today; and this despite the fact that, with us, the amazing advance and excellence of medical knowledge and skill have restricted the need of cures by other than scientific means.

MIRACLES AND DIVINE HEALING

In the third place, therefore, we have to recognise that the Church is not empowered to work New Testament miracles as a normal part of its Healing Ministry. Despite the revived interest in Divine Healing during the past half-century; despite, also, the present extensive practice of Spiritual Healing in its manifold and varied forms—yet comparatively few cases of bodily cures effected apart from medical science can be substantiated.

In seeking, therefore, to assess the truth regarding miraculous cures wrought apart from medical science, and which medical science cannot explain, there are four considerations to be borne in mind:

First, medical science is ready (and to my mind over-ready) to explain, or explain away, every miraculous cure, either as wrong diagnosis, or mistaken prognosis, or temporary remission, or (as a last resort) spontaneous recovery. Though inexplicable cures form a relatively inconsiderable proportion of all recoveries from sickness, yet there are undoubtedly a sufficient number of them in which Divine Healing has played a part to establish a definite connection between the two—Divine Healing and miraculous cure.

25

Secondly, every variety of authenticated cure claimed by Divine Healing can be paralleled (to quote the words of Canon L. W. Grensted, D.D.) "by equally miraculous recoveries, which, if not spontaneous, are the result of teaching and practice which range from auto-suggestion to sub-Christian magic": even as was the case in sub-Apostolic days.

Thirdly, it is almost impossible to exaggerate the power of auto-suggestion. At the same time, auto-suggestion based on the almighty power of God becomes a spiritual force and far more potent than when based on self-reliance or the skill of a fallible doctor.

Finally, a healing power possessed by some people, and supposed in the past to be a charismatic gift, is now recognised as a physical, not a spiritual, endowment, and capable of scientific explanation, investigation, and development.

We all possess a *Vis Mediatrix Naturae*, a natural healing energy, which accounts, for example, for the closing and healing of wounds. There are those who can transmit this force or energy to a patient. It explains the healing fingers of professional healers which convey what patients describe as an electric shock from the one to the other. It may even explain our Lord's statement that "virtue had gone out" of Him, when the woman with an issue of blood touched the hem of His garment. But it is no more a spiritual grace than the rays of an infra-red lamp, or the intuition of an osteopath—though it is none the less a divinely bestowed faculty because it can be scientifically investigated and employed.

New Testament Miracles

It is evident from this short review of miraculous healing that the Church cannot substantiate a claim to dispense with medical healing by reason of miraculous powers transmitted to it by Christ. This can only mean that the miracles of the Gospels and of the Acts are in an entirely different category from subsequent non-medical healing, whether practised within or without the Church.

In the first place, we notice that they were, for the most part, immediate cures—such as occur so seldom even in cases of spontaneous recovery.

Then, also, New Testament miracles were, in so many cases, outside the province in which subsequent Divine Healing has sought to operate. They include the raising of the dead; the restoration of a severed ear; and would any "healer" or any doctor in his surgery feel competent to deal with a collection of patients which a medical practitioner has described as "a man born blind, a dumb epileptic, a woman with severe curvature of the spine, a man with old infantile paralysis causing the wasting of an arm, two or three persons who were stone deaf, a paralytic of thirty-eight years' standing, and a couple of raving lunatics"? Spastics, morons, and the limbless could all have looked to Christ to have been made whole.

The New Testament miracles evidently find their explanation in the Person of Christ Himself. As John Fisher wrote in 1828, in his *Rise and Progress of Religion*, our Lord's "miracles were the tolling of the great bell of the Universe to call attention to the sermon that was to follow". That sermon was not the good news of the bodily healing of all and sundry, but the Gospel of the salvation of the whole man, Eternal Life, and the Church He was founding to continue His ministry of redemption. The Saviour Himself termed His miracles "signs", to prove His identity as the expected Messiah or Christ of God. And He bequeathed the power of their operation to His Apostles, to be (in the words of Archbishop Trench) "the swaddling clothes of the infant Church, till it had learned to walk".

So it is that St. Paul, as he watched the gradual disappearance of the early charismatic gifts of the Church (listed at the conclusion of 1 Corinthians 12—Miracles, Gifts of Healing, Prophesyings, and Tongues), pointed, in the following chapter,

27

to the more excellent and abiding gift of the Holy Spirit, the gift of love.

THE WHOLE MAN AND WHOLENESS

We are now in a position to examine *de novo*, with impartial minds, our Lord's commission to the Church to heal the sick, and the special function of the Church in the general ministry of Divine Healing.

St. Matthew's Gospel in two places (4: 23 and 9: 35) summarises our Lord's earthly ministry as follows: "Jesus went about all the cities and the villages *teaching* in their synagogues, and *preaching* the gospel of the kingdom, and *healing* all manner of disease and all manner of sickness." Such repetition shows (it is thought) that the Evangelist is here quoting from the earliest of catechisms, compiled by the Apostles themselves, to describe the mission of their Master. That mission was, thus, to seek and to save the *whole* man—mind (teaching), spirit (preaching) and body (healing). Similarly, our Lord's commission to His Church was the salvation of the whole man. The Church was to be the extension of the Incarnation, the Body of Christ going "about doing good" (Acts 10: 38).

What, then, is man? Psychologists teach that man is a complicated and interacting amalgam of body, mind and spirit, and it is now recognised that healing cannot be confined to curing disease; it is to restore the whole man, the person. The truest definition of health is wholeness, even as it is the derivation of the word. Healing is thus seen to be the restoration of wholeness; and to be made whole must include the mind and the spirit in the cure as well as the body. It is therefore increasingly recognised that the co-operation of the doctor, the psychiatrist and the priest is required in this one Christian ministry of human redemption or of recovery of wholeness. From this it follows that:

On the one hand, the doctor and the psychiatrist are included in our Lord's commission to His Church to heal the sick. For this reason the bishops, generally, are agreed that Christian doctors

28

and psychiatrists have as clear a title to be ordained as have the teachers of secular subjects in schools and universities.

On the other hand, the medical profession should call in the aid of parish priests and chaplains as a normal practice. As the recent Memorandum on Divine Healing by the Committee of the British Medical Association emphasises: "Team-work between doctor and clergyman can help to meet the *total* needs of the patient."

The need for such co-operation will be evident if illness is divided into the three types of Psychosomatic Disorder, Organic Disorders, and (so called) Hopeless Cases; and we enquire to what extent Spiritual Healing can contribute to the cure of the sufferer regarded as a person, not as a case.

DIVINE HEALING AND PSYCHOSOMATIC DISORDER

First, psychosomatic disorder. As the term implies, psychosomatic disorder has its origin in the spirit of man. Duodenal ulcers are almost invariably the result of worry. Certain forms of rheumatism can be occasioned by unrecognised resentment, nervous indigestion by anxiety. As, therefore, the seat of disorder is in the realm of the spirit, so also must be the restoration of order and wholeness.

Such patients can, of course, be healed by psychotherapy— and satisfactorily so up to a point. But as a recent article on "Freud and Religion" (*Sunday Observer*, 27th May, 1956) confessed: "All psychotherapists recognise that, even after complete and successful analysis, the subject has still no more than his own individual resources on which to draw. And in fact these are sometimes not enough." So it is that Professor C. G. Jung, in his *Man in Search of a Soul*, declares that: "Among all my patients in the second half of life, that is over thirty-five, there has not been one whose problem in the last resort was not one of finding a religious outlook on life. It is safe to say that every one of them fell ill because he had lost that which the living religions of every age have given to their

29

followers, and none of them has been really healed who did not regain his religious outlook."

DIVINE HEALING AND ORGANIC DISORDER

Secondly, what part does Divine Healing play in cases of organic disorder? In all illness the chief hindrance to recovery is fear. With such mental anxiety Divine Healing is directly concerned. For the professed and primary purpose of Divine Healing is to bring the sufferer into a condition of utter trust and confidence in the wisdom, power and love of God our heavenly Father, who doeth all things well. Such trust and confidence in a Personal God removes fear and anxiety from the mind; and once the love of God has banished all bedevilling fear, then the way is open for bodily restoration. Indeed, where man's spirit is in conscious and tranquil union with God in Christ there is no limit to the infusion of healing power that can permeate every cell of the sufferer's body, effecting astonishing recovery.

There is, however, this all-important qualification: "if God so will"; which is inherent in a belief in a Personal God who is Wisdom, Power and Love. The *Love of God* is profoundly concerned for the highest welfare of the whole man, the person, of every one of his children—not simply for our bodily ease. The *Power of God* is able to heal and to save and to enable to the uttermost. But the *Wisdom of God* may know, as we cannot know, that even as gold is refined in the fire, so an immortal being may be better fitted for influence here and special responsibility in the real life hereafter, if some bodily disorder remains unhealed.

Scripture, indeed, gives no warrant for the assumption that as a God of Love cannot "will" pain and suffering for His children, therefore the only requisite for full recovery in every case is sufficient faith on the part of the patient, or the priest, or the patient's friends, or the Church at large. Gethsemane is the efficient answer, in this life, to the mysterious problem of evil in God's good world. The first of the three prayers of the Agony in the Garden was one of *pleading*: "Let this cup pass from me." The second prayer was one of *resignation*: "If this cup may not pass away from me except I drink it, Thy will be done." After the third prayer came *triumphant acceptance*, with the Saviour marching forward to meet His arrest, crying: "The cup which my Father hath given me, shall I not drink it?" Moreover, even as the Father could not have "willed" the Cross for His beloved Son, and yet He overruled its shameful wickedness to be the salvation of the world, so He can likewise overrule suffering, which He never willed, to the greater glory of the sufferer in this world, and for promotion to offices of peculiar honour in the life of the world to come.

We live in an evil and unsafe world, which only a pre-cosmic fall can partially explain. Though, therefore, God's *primary* purpose is the health and happiness of the human race, yet He has a *secondary* purpose—namely, to overrule suffering for the redemption of the world. In that travailing redemption, sufferers are privileged to find themselves partakers with Christ (1 Pet. 4: 13), even as St. Paul rejoiced that he was, in some sense, mysteriously allowed to fill up, on his part, that which was lacking of the afflictions of Christ (Col. 1: 24).

DIVINE HEALING AND HOPELESS CASES

Finally, under this category, I include cases where Divine Healing has effected a cure, or an alleviation, beyond the skill or understanding of medical science. As was made manifest by the Incarnation, when the fullness of the Godhead moved among men and healed their sick, the wisdom, power and love of God can intervene to work miracles of bodily recovery. Why it is His good pleasure thus to intervene in some cases and not in others is a baffling problem that awaits our fuller knowledge. All preparation for Divine Healing must begin with the clear explanation that bodily restoration is not always God's answer to prayer for wholeness of personality, nor is it the primary purpose of placing the sufferer in conscious communion with a heavenly Father of wisdom, power and love.

Thus, it is profoundly wrong to suppose that failure in recovery is due to lack of faith. God's intervention in response to prayer does not depend entirely upon the faith of the *patient*: and it is cruel for a healer to add the septic sting of reproach to acute disappointment by attributing non-recovery to this cause.

Neither does God's intervention depend on the faith of the *healer*; the laying on of hands and holy unction are sacramental in character and the priest is only the agent for conveying the healing power of Almighty God. At the same time, some priests, as also some lay-people, are more gifted than others in communicating the sense of the love and presence of God to sufferers, and in placing them in the conscious safety and contentment of the everlasting arms of our Eternal Refuge. Both in Ephesians (chap. 4) and 1 Corinthians (chap. 13) St. Paul emphasises the diversity of Christ's gifts to His Church.

In so far as faith mysteriously qualifies for God's intervention to be vouchsafed, it is the faith of the *whole Church* that offers to God the human co-operation that is essential if He is to work His miracles of grace and healing. For, "man can do nothing without God, and God will do nothing without man". The Gospel illustration of the co-operation of the Church is the healing of the man sick of the palsy, "borne of four", where faith smashed through a roof to lay their friend on his bed at the feet of the Saviour when the passage-ways were blocked with a thronging crowd from Capernaum (Mark 2: 1–12). In this essential qualification of the "prayer of faith" that saves the sick (Jas. 5: 15) it is important to recognise the difference between magic and religion. *Magic* is to seek to bend God's will to our human will. *Religion* is to bend our wills to God's almighty will. The "prayer of faith", therefore, must never be considered as willing God to effect a miracle, after the manner of the priests of Baal on Mount Carmel. Rather, it is to seek to co-operate with God in the fulfilment of His purposes of

wisdom, power and love. For this healing ministry of intercession the Church should, more particularly, mobilise its
great army of house-bound and bed-ridden invalids, providing
them with cases for whom to pray and keeping them informed
when they can co-operate from their own homes in healing
services that have been arranged in the Church or in sick-rooms.

HEALING SERVICES

Thus, finally, there is the controversial issue of healing services.
Experience is showing the danger of great healing services, to
which all and sundry receive a general invitation without the
due preparation of each sufferer. The mass emotion and
hysteria thereby engendered may be gravely unhealthy. On
the other hand, many clergy have proved abundantly the value
of a group of intercessors who meet for imaginative prayer.
Bid the intercessors to "go into the ward (or to the bedside)
and stand with Christ next to the bed. Believe that at this very
moment Christ is touching the life of the sufferer . . . and that
He can more powerfully work in the atmosphere of our faith
and love". The results are quite remarkable, even when no
bodily healing results. Another practice of certain clergy is,
each week, or at less frequent intervals, to lay their hands on
one or more patients who have been carefully prepared, while
an interceding congregation is gathered in the church. It is,
indeed, along such lines that the Ministry of Divine Healing is
at present being chiefly pursued as the Church humbly seeks
to explore the merciful riches of the wisdom, power and love of
almighty God, our heavenly Father.

In conclusion, from all that has gone before, two truths stand
forth on which practical action can be taken with immense
benefit:

1. As the Committee of the British Medical Association
stress in their Report, the need of doctors, psychiatrists and
parish priests (or hospital chaplains), co-operating together

to heal the whole person, has never been more fully recognised. In the words of Professor Sir Cyril Burt, the patient "is something more than a carcase loosely coupled with a ghost". Thus, Divine Healing is the co-operation of God's medical and spiritual ministries as ordained by Him from the beginning.

2. There is the requirement of the interceding congregation co-operating with the bedside ministry of the parish priest. The Divine Healing that results is one more instance that "more things are wrought by prayer than this world dreams of".

2

DIVINE HEALING AS A DOCTOR SEES IT

by DR. J. BURNETT RAE

Following his training at Aberdeen and some time in general practice, Dr. Burnett Rae, M.B., Ch.B., has specialised in Psychological Medicine, and is an Honorary Consultant Physician at Croydon General Hospital, and a Fellow of the Royal Society of Medicine. He has always been keenly interested in promoting co-operation between the Medical profession and the Church, and is Vice-Chairman of the Churches' Council of Healing. He has written many articles on Divine Healing, including Spiritual Healing—A Doctor's Comment.

HEALTH AND HEALING have always been an integral part of the Christian message, and is this to be wondered at? Who is there who does not know how disturbing a thing disease of any kind can be? All is going well in a family; life is ordered and happy; suddenly, like a bolt from the blue, illness comes into the home, the husband or wife is struck down and work is stopped, and the means of livelihood affected. Life in consequence is terribly changed, and not only for the family or individual concerned but for many others—for industry, for the State. It was estimated recently that ten million working hours had been lost to industry in one year through functional nervous diseases alone.

This is a problem which affects us all. No one can contract out of it. We are all involved in the possibility and problem of disease. Health is not merely an endowment, something we are given or not given; it is an achievement. To be healthy, one must be growing more and more healthy; to be well, one must always be getting better. This principle applies to all ages and stages of life. Even when the body is growing old, in the autumn of its days, the mind and the spirit should still be growing; as "our outward man" perishes, "our inward man" should be "renewed day by day". To be static is dangerous. A cancer is part of the body that is not growing as it should; it is regressing—going back to the primitive.

There is an impulse in man to grow up, to develop and express his true nature, the instincts and faculties with which he has been endowed. If through lack of opportunity, or ignorance, or a feeling of inadequacy, this urge of life is frustrated and turns inward, something which was good becomes sour and bad.

The higher up the biological scale we go, the more we find this impulse becoming purposeful and intelligent, until in man we are aware of a spirit that can co-operate with the Spirit of all life, with the Creator who knows better than we what life is for, and how the health and the healing of the individual and the nation are to be achieved.

Recently a patient came to see me at my hospital. She was depressed and had lost all interest in her work and home; she was much worried in consequence and could not sleep. An additional worry was the fact that her doctor had told her there was nothing fundamentally wrong with her. I had to explain that what he really meant was that there was nothing organically wrong with her body. In view of the fact that she had lost all joy of living, the real question was whether there was anything fundamentally right.

Health, we are beginning to realise, is not just a physical matter. The body certainly has a tremendous influence upon the mind; "We are not ourselves," says Shakespeare, "when nature, being oppressed, commands the mind to suffer with the body." Every day we notice how physical ill-health can affect not only the mentality but even the spiritual outlook of an individual. This is one of the most painful tragic facts of human life, and for this reason a Gospel of Salvation, if it is to be adequate, must be concerned—and potent—to heal the body as well as the soul.

But if the body affects the mind, the mind has a great influence upon the body. I specialise in the psychological side of medicine; and if medical psychology has done anything, it has exploded the idea that a man can be divided into sections which have nothing to do with each other. It has shown decisively that health is not just a matter of the body, or of the mind, but of the essential unity of both. For health we require good food, fresh air, sufficient rest, exercise, and work. Man does not live by bread alone; food for the mind, intellectual interests, and all the things that refresh the spirit are just as necessary. "Better a dinner of herbs where love is, than a stalled ox and hatred therewith" (Prov. 15: 17). It is indeed a better dinner; it does you more good. "A merry heart doeth good like a medicine, but a broken spirit drieth up the bones" (Prov. 17: 22). Perfectly true, and therefore we must unite and not keep apart these two aspects of our nature. Elijah, after his battle with the priests of Baal, wanted to die; he felt he was no better than his fathers, not up to his job—a clear case of nervous exhaustion. When asleep under the juniper tree, he had a dream in which he was told by an angel to rise and eat, which he did. He required food; but it was because he believed that an angel had prescribed it—that God had a care for him—that he was able to go in the strength of that food for forty days (1 Kings 19).

We separate too much the physical and the spiritual. They are different—that which is born of the flesh is flesh, and that which is born of the spirit is spirit—but they are related and have need of each other. What God has joined together let not man put asunder. It is a right trend on the part of medical science to regard the body and the mind, not as separate, but as different aspects of one unity. St. Paul prayed that the Thessalonians might be sanctified wholly by the God of peace; that spirit, soul and body might be preserved entire.

A very striking illustration of this interdependence is given in the report of St. Mark on the healing of the paralysed man who was let in through the roof. The patient came to be cured of a physical malady, and the first thing that happened was an assurance that his sins were forgiven. It must have seemed both to the patient and to his friends a somewhat irrelevant observation; some also thought it irreverent and blasphemous, and questioned Christ's authority. Then the procedure was reversed. Instead of an argument, they were given a demonstration: "That ye may know that the Son of man hath power on earth to forgive sins (He said to the sick of the palsy), I say unto thee, Arise, and take up thy bed and go thy way into thine house" (Mark 2: 10). It is clear that Christ, if He was not justifying His moral authority by a physical action, was at any rate pointing out that a separation must not be made between the one realm and the other.

Similarly, we do not feel that there is anything arbitrary or out of place in Christ's miracles; they seem to follow naturally in the wake of His personality. The inner life is that which gives significance and value to the outer life, which is usually a good test of the truth and validity of the inner.

The external world is the stage on which we have to play our role in the great drama; and we are well cast for our part, if only we bring to it the energy and the vision which the inner life supplies. Here, as elsewhere, it is true that what we get out of anything depends very largely on what we bring to it. We are too apt to confuse reality with externality, to suppose that the real world is the world that we can see or handle or assess. The reality of a flower for us is not just the flower but what its beauty and fragrance mean for us; it depends quite as much on what we bring to the flower as what it brings to us. It needs, as Lotze has said, "the sentient mind of man to discover what it is mutely striving to express". As we get older we become less dependent upon external sources of enjoyment and find these more in ourselves. Lacordaire says finely that the inner life is the conversation of oneself with oneself:

"Every man has this word within which makes his life true: it is this inner life which makes the whole valour of the man. There goes one in a purple cloak who is only a miserable because the word which he says to himself is the word of a miserable; and there going down the street is a beggar who is a great man because the word which he says to himself is the word of a hero or a saint."

Psychological medicine affords ample confirmation of all this. At a clinic which I attended for the scientific treatment of delinquency, some of the cases are classified under the term "behaviour problems"; and most of these can be traced not only to physical but to emotional and mental causes.

Let me quote what Sir Henry Cohen, an ex-President of the B.M.A., said in his presidential address at the annual meeting of the Association:

"Medicine is not all science. There are many medical problems which defy measurement. Human life is full of imponderables, for man is not a physical being only. He has emotions and appetites which cannot be measured, though they profoundly influence his physical welfare. Bodily disturbances may be, and commonly are, the expression of his loves and hates, his passions and fears, his worries and anxieties; the thumping heart, the cold sweat, the weak and tremulous knees of fright are but simple examples of this unity of body and mind. The greatest danger to which medicine in the scientific era has been exposed is that of overlooking that men, both patients and doctors, are sentient social beings, and of forgetting that, however sensitive and specific our laboratory tests, and however elaborate and complicated our instrumental methods of investigation may be, they are not ends in themselves."

Again, Dr. Walshe, at the conclusion of his Linacre Lecture to the fellows of St. John's College, Cambridge, said: "The practice of medicine flourishes most when doctors remember that prudence governs the employment of science, and that in the last resort they are concerned with the ultimate particular thing, the human person, whom science by itself is inadequate to comprehend."

In these passages I discern a feeling that is humble and expectant, a desire for the help that must come from those who are searching for truth and healing in a different category of human experience, help such as the Christian religion should be able to provide.

This is a new outlook in medicine. When I began medical practice the idea that the mind and spirit had any real effect upon health or disease was not seriously entertained, and one still comes across old-fashioned people who think like that.

Some time ago I had to treat a professor—a Senior Wrangler—whose faith in anything physical, in a pill or a potion, was almost pathetic; but when I suggested that his trouble might be due to a wrong mental attitude he was quite incredulous and looked at me as if he thought I had mistaken my profession. But this attitude is passing rapidly.

Frequently we meet with those who go to the other extreme and think that all disease is purely mental in origin, and who do not approve of any remedy of a physical nature. This some-times leads to strange conclusions. When I offered a prescrip-tion to one lady she said firmly, "No. I never take drugs. If I have indigestion, I just take some bicarbonate of soda, a little sal volatile and ten drops of tincture of ginger!"

But we must not overlook the difficulties. The fact is that when it comes to actual practice, the religious and the scientific points of view are very different and even seem to conflict. A few years ago in the columns of *The Lancet* a very interesting correspondence took place. Professor Platt, the well-known orthopaedic surgeon in Manchester, writing on *The Doctor's Creed*, in reply to an address which had been given by the Archbishop of Canterbury, said that while he accepted the Christian ethic, he could not accept Christian doctrine—he had seen too many children die of nephritis to believe that God could be both good and all-powerful.

It was interesting to note that his letter was followed by a flood of correspondence from other doctors—in all branches of medicine—dissociating themselves from this conclusion and pointing out that Christianity without Christ was both illogical and impossible. They recognised that the problem of goodness is just as great as that of evil; that Professor Platt, demanding a high ethic and refusing any deity who was not good, was himself a problem as great as the evil and suffering of the world which he deplored. The doctors were on the side of the angels and the archbishop! But what I failed to notice was any attempt to show the necessity for religion in actual medical practice. They seemed content to keep their science in one compartment of life and their religion in another. This is not Christianity. Religion is not a duty, but something which has to do with *all* duties. "To spiritualize what is material, to Christianize what is secular—this is the noble achievement of Christian principle."

The Churches' Council of Healing is an inter-denominational council of doctors, clergy and laymen which seeks to provide a common basis for the healing movements which stand on Christian foundations, and to afford a recognised basis for the co-operation of doctors and clergy in the study and performance of their respective functions in the work of healing. It is a federating body seeking to support and unite the various guilds which, for some time now, have been concerned both with health and healing, and to bring all these into closer relation with the work of the Church. The Council has won the support of the British Medical Association, who have appointed representatives to serve on its Executive. This is a notable, I would say historic, event. It means that there is a recognition on the part of the medical profession that faith and reason must go hand in hand in the work of healing; that the whole nature of man—body, mind and spirit—must be evoked if health in the full sense of the word is to be attained and maintained.

Now, if health is wholeness—the functional unity of the organism and of personality—there must be some unifying factor to bring it about, to hold together the elements in our nature which otherwise might be contradictory rather than complementary. All healthy life grows out from a centre in its being. In the case of man, I discover this in what we call the soul, for this is the link between the spiritual and the physical aspects of our nature.

Psychology is the science of the soul. If we think of it today rather as the science of the mind, or of mental behaviour, then the *whole* mind must be taken into account—the conscious, the subconscious, and the super-conscious. When we are referring to all these there is much to be said for retaining the term soul as a better description of what we mean. It is here that the diverse interests of flesh and spirit meet and influence each other. If for any reason this link is lost or weakened, there is no through way for the forces of the spirit to reach the body, and that must spell weakness. This can go so far as to produce an actual split in consciousness, which we call schizophrenia. Short of that, there may be anxiety, fear, and all the mental and physical effects which result from this. These are the cases where shock therapy is sometimes employed, and it can be helpful; but it is obvious that it is of little use shocking or pulling a person together into a state of reality if he cannot stay there.

Our Lord attached the greatest importance to the value of the human soul. "What shall it profit a man if he gains the whole world and lose his own soul" (Mark 8: 36). It is in the soul, says Maeterlinck, that the great things happen. Here are born those intuitions which we have for that which is good and true and lovely; here we come into touch with that which is real. The soul seems to have a magnetic power drawing to itself what it needs from the world outside, and giving what is in its nature to give.

Earlier in this essay I mentioned the universal urge that there is in living things to express their instincts and faculties according to their particular nature, seeking a fuller life beyond. This is essential to health and applies both to our physical and spiritual nature. But it is just here that we come up against a fact which must be taken into account: it is the fact of evil, the fact that something has gone wrong with our human nature. So we find Berdyaev, the Russian philosopher, describing man as a contradictory being, God-like and beast-like, free and enslaved, capable of great love and sacrifice, capable also of great cruelty and unlimited egoism. It is because he cannot resolve this conflict that he is afraid—afraid of the evil and afraid also of the good, of the devil and also of God.

If this description be true, is there not need for spiritual healing? Must man not be healed in his body and spirit? The psychiatrist spends much of his time going to the cause of his patient's difficulty, believing that if he can discover this the patient will himself be able to deal with it. There is a measure of truth in that, because knowledge increases our opportunity of deriving profit from our own thought and exertion; but at the best it is often a half-truth. We may know very well the cause of our trouble and yet be unable to deal with it. What we really need is a power to overcome it, to do the hard, uninteresting duty, to defeat the degrading fear or resentment.

This is not just the problem of the neurotic; it is the problem of the human race. Who has not deplored at times the ineffectiveness of the human intellect to do, not only what it ought to do, but what it really wants to do? Like the Apostle, the patient sees a law in his members warring against the law of his mind and bringing him into captivity. "I know that this fear of mine is wrong and stupid, and I hate and despise it; but it defeats me every time." Who in some measure cannot endorse that patient's statement? And often it is the very irrationality of the fear or the folly which is so devastating.

The Christian solution is that alongside this fact of sin and evil comes the fact of God, not only to forgive, but to heal. When man finds that he is forgiven, he is aware also that he is being healed. In Christ we have reason to expect both—that

God, who "forgiveth all our iniquities, healeth all our diseases".

In our day there is apparent a notable increase in mental and nervous disorders, many of them of a purely functional character, but none the less distressing and serious on that account. Many drugs are being put on the medical market with a view to putting a barrier between the patient and the source of his worries, anxieties and obsessions. This may have a real value in certain cases, but to be incapable of pain or anxiety would itself be a serious disorder. We should rise above anxiety, not fall below it. When the Apostle, writing to the Philippians (4: 5-6) said, "In nothing be anxious", he preceded that advice by saying, "The Lord is at hand". Apart from that, it would have been a very trite remark. To meet the thousand shocks that flesh is heir to, both from without and from within, God is needed.

It is certainly easier in many ways to keep our science and religion apart, but the healing of the sick and the preaching of the Gospel must go together. There are spiritual healers who are concerned to revive the Ministry of Healing as it was in the early days of the Church. This is impossible; we must go forward, recognising all that we have learnt since those early days, and being led by the spirit of truth into all that awaits us in the future. The Church cannot ignore the advance of science, physical and mental. It is no less true that a purely intellectual approach to the problem of suffering must fail. The influence of the spiritual upon the mental is quite as necessary as that of the mind upon the body.

As a doctor I have dealt mainly with the human side of our subject. There is this side to it; without the effort of the patient or of his friends—whatever means have been employed—we cannot envisage Spiritual Healing. But this is not the only aspect of the matter, nor is it the most important. We may try too little, but we may try too much, and in this way put a check upon the movement of the divine. Who has not noticed that often it was when he came to the end of his own resources and was on the brink of despair, when he had no choice but to throw himself without reserve upon the grace and healing power of God, that something was done for him which he could never have done for himself? The door seemed to open of its own accord.

It seems as if a transference of thought and feeling and will must take place before that greater flow from the divine to the human can occur. Then healing happens—something a doctor can observe but can never explain, for its reality is to be discovered not in the body, nor in the mind, but in the Spirit, in that which never was on land or sea, but which once moved on the face of the waters, creating both mind and body, making all things new.[1]

[1] Reproduced by kind permission of the Editor of *The London Quarterly and Holborn Review*.

3

SOME PROBLEMS RAISED BY DIVINE HEALING

by THE VERY REV. H. C. ROBINS

As Dean of Sarum, 1945–52, our contributor did much to promote the Healing Ministry of the Church in the Salisbury Diocese, and he is well known for his book A Guide to Spiritual Healing. *He has exercised a devoted pastoral ministry in the South of England, serving as Vicar of Romford 1922–30, Barking 1930–35 and Portsea 1935–43.*

IN WRITING about the problems of Divine Healing it is well first to make quite clear what one means by Spiritual or Divine Healing. I mean, first, healing by the direct action of God without surgery or drugs, but using spiritual means such as prayer, unction and the laying on of hands. But I also mean the co-operation of the Church and doctors, in which each side has its specific part to play in what is, or should be, a joint undertaking. It is clear that the modern revival of what was almost, but never quite, a lost function of the Church, and the increasing interest in that revival taken by many ordinary people, raises many problems both intellectual and practical. I shall confine myself mainly to the intellectual and theological issues.

The first and most fundamental problem to be raised is: Is disease God's will, or sent by Him? The importance of this question cannot possibly be exaggerated, for (1) it involves the very character of God Himself, and therefore of the very nature of the universe. If I really believed that cancer was deliberately sent by God as a fatherly visitation I do not think I could continue to believe in Him as my Heavenly Father. I might still believe in a Supreme Being, but not in a God of perfect Love. (2) The belief that it is GOD's will constitutes a severe obstacle to healing, for we should presumably resign ourselves to it and should hardly send for a doctor to try and remove something sent by God! And, indeed, doctors would lose the very *raison d'être* of their profession. (3) The continued assertion is in part responsible for the drift away to various heretical sects of many devout Christians because it convinces them that they cannot obtain the help which they desperately need, and should be reasonably confident of finding within the Church.

This problem is vital, but it is by no means easy to answer. My general line of reply is that disease is not God's will, though He permits it. Let us look at the evidence. The Old Testament is very confused. You can quote statements for and against sickness being regarded as sent by God, but its main trend is that it is sent by Him. This is, I think, due to the profound sense of the Jewish mind as to the majesty of God, which led them to ascribe almost everything that happens to His omnipotent will. The New Testament takes the opposite view. If you examine the activity of Our Lord Himself this is abundantly clear. For (1) He never ascribes sickness to God, but quite often to Satan, whose works He came to destroy. He does indeed imply that its healing may be to the Glory of God, but this is very different from saying that God sends it. (2) He Himself continually claimed that He came to DO His Father's will. Why then did He spend so much of His ministry in healing sickness if it is God's will? And why did He send out the twelve and the seventy with the solemn commission not only to preach the Gospel but to heal the sick? Why did He commission His Church to continue His healing ministry, promising them the ability to do even greater works than His own? (3) If sickness is God's will, how could He point to His works of healing as proof that He was the Coming One when questioned by John's disciples? (4) It is very nearly if not quite

47

impossible to square the view that sickness is God's will with His revelation of God as perfect Love and as our Heavenly Father. The rest of the New Testament offers a background to Our Lord's teaching. In the Acts, St. Peter and St. Paul not only preached but healed, as a definite part of their ministry. In 1 Corinthians 12 healing is mentioned as one of the "Gifts of the Spirit" and there is of course the classic commendation of healing in the 5th chapter of St. James's epistle. The only possible evidence that sickness may be sent by God is St. Paul's "thorn in the flesh", some physical disability, which in spite of St. Paul's earnest prayer, God did not remove. But it is significant that St. Paul calls it not a fatherly visitation of God, but a "messenger of Satan to buffet me". The general impression left by the New Testament is not of sickness as God's will but of our Lord and His Church strongly combating something that is definitely contrary to God's will.

What are we to say as to the Book of Common Prayer? We are bound to admit that it speaks with a very uncertain and equivocal voice. The Visitation and the Communion of the Sick in the 1662 Book imply, and even assert, that sickness is God's fatherly chastisement, and are so lugubrious that they are the last thing in the world with which I should wish to be confronted in illness! The 1928 Proposed Book is much better, and takes a much more positive standpoint. But even this book in one of the prayers for the sick in the "Occasional Prayers" takes away much of its positive content by qualifying its petition for healing with "if it be Thy gracious will". Such in brief is the evidence, but for myself I can only say that, difficult as it is, I believe that it is more truly Christian and in accordance with the New Testament to assert that sickness is *not* God's will. People defend the opposite point of view by asserting that sickness is a means to sanctification. I would not deny that God may use it to this end, but this is not to say that He definitely wills it. And we should not forget that it often has precisely the opposite effect!

But if we deny that sickness is God's will we are still left to face the problem: What then is its origin? It is not possible to give a completely satisfactory answer, as the question is bound up with the problem of evil which is insoluble in this life. But we can at least attempt a partial answer along these lines: (1) We can ascribe it, as our Lord does, to man's adversary the Devil. It is not very fashionable nowadays to believe in a personal devil, and indeed we have to beware of a dualistic conception of the universe. But two world wars have driven us to the idea of demonic forces of evil at work in the world, and we might even make play with the idea of a pre-cosmic fall and kink in the world as set forth by Dr. N. P. Williams in his *Bampton Lectures*. (2) We may find its origin in the abuse of the measure of free-will and self-determination given by God to man. In giving man free-will God had to take the risk that man would abuse His gift. This risk God took, because the alternative was a physically perfect but loveless universe, as love to be love must be free. (3) We may find the origin of disease in the sin and ignorance that have followed the abuse of our freedom and which have put man out of harmony with God and His laws of health. Sometimes it is the sin of the individual. If a man is a glutton or a drunkard he will suffer for it. As psychosomatic medicine is pointing out to us, the root cause of illness lies in the mind and spirit, in the fears, resentments, envies, unrepented sin and even the perhaps unrecognised desire to continue ill and so be the centre of attention, and avoid the necessity of facing life. Here the fault lies in ourselves. But more often it lies in the general sin and ignorance of humanity, which have thrown mankind out of harmony with God and His laws of health. Here is the root of disease: that humanity has lost touch with God.

Another problem is the influence of spirit and mind upon body. The mind has two levels: the conscious, of which we are aware; and the subconscious, the seat of our instincts and instinctive emotions and race consciousness. Psychologists tell us that, just as the submerged part of an iceberg is far larger than what is visible, so the subconscious part of our mind is of far greater extent than that of which we are aware. It is this which goes on working when our conscious mind is asleep. And it is this subconscious which is the engineer-in-charge of our bodily functions. We do not, for example, say, "Now let us breathe." The subconscious sees to that for us. The problem arises because our subconscious mind is terribly suggestible, and is open to suggestions from our own and other minds: but still more from the fact that it is utterly uncritical, and will accept and act on any suggestion good or bad, negative or positive, provided it is strong enough.

The trouble is that the suggestions we send down to our subconscious are so often bad and negative. Take the periodic influenza scares which sweep the country. You perhaps feel a trifle off colour; you meet a friend who says, "You do not look too good, and I hear Mrs. Robinson is in bed." You open your newspaper and read of outbreaks and mounting percentages. Finally your very suggestible subconscious says, "Well, everyone expects me to catch it. It is the thing to do." And catch it you do. Or, take that most annoying of all banes, sleeplessness. Was it not Bishop Michael Furse who said to a sufferer, "You go upstairs saying despondently, Now for another of those sleepless nights, and your subconscious sees that you get one." The doctor whose mind is full of positive thoughts of service to the afflicted, sleeps well after a hard day's work and normally escapes influenza. If only we could persuade ourselves to feed the subconscious with cheerful, positive suggestions, how much wiser and healthier we should be.

Or take the case of undealt-with sin. If we fail to repent, it festers as a complex in the subconscious, and quite often shows itself in physical symptoms of disease. So it is very important to avoid negative thinking and to drive out the negative by the positive, thus in time overcoming evil with good. For "as a man thinketh in his heart, so is he" (Prov. 23: 7).

Another problem is: What is to be the attitude of the orthodox Christian to heretical sects and healers? Their name is legion, for they are many. They are springing up like mushrooms both in this country and in the United States of America, and for the Christian they raise acute problems both intellectual and practical—intellectual, because we have to see the points on which we agree and those from which we differ; practical because they do certainly effect cures, and also because many orthodox Christians are drifting away to them from their proper spiritual affiliations, seeking the help they could and should find in the Church. I have neither the time nor the knowledge to deal with them all. But I wish to say a few words about Christian Science. The old cliché is probably true that it is neither Christian nor scientific. It has of course some truth in it, e.g. the assertion of the love of God and the effect of mind upon body. But, like most heresies, it takes a truth and pushes it so far that it becomes untruth. So keen is it to emphasise "good" and "mind" that it practically denies the reality both of evil and the material body. This would do away with the Incarnation, the manifestation of God in a human body, and is indeed nonsense. Evil is not so real as good, but common sense should convince us of its dread reality. Those who deny the reality of evil are like someone standing out in a thundershower and getting drenched while he complacently remarks, "Of course it is not real rain." And Christian Science is both foolish and unrealistic in its frequent refusal to accept the help of medical science.

If one considers the Spiritualists one need not deny that they do in some cases effect a cure. But I can only view with incredulity their claim to work by the dubious technique of mediums, controls and departed spirits. Furthermore, I feel bound to sound a warning note against the practice of many heretical sects of holding widely publicised, imperfectly prepared and highly emotional mass healing services. These may bring healing, often only temporary, to suggestible patients, but bring disappointment and disillusionment to the vast majority. No, the Christian sufferer is wise to stick to the Church with its ancient and Biblical methods of prayer, unction and the laying on of hands. These are well tried and will not be found wanting.

Another urgent theological problem is presented by the need to study the working of the spiritual laws of the universe. One thing is clear beyond a shadow of doubt: that man's exploration of spiritual law has not kept pace with his daily increasing knowledge of physical or natural law. Almost literally day by day we discover more and more about the physical conditions of our material world. To take only two examples. We have learnt how to split the atom, and have released vast realms of atomic power with its boundless and incalculable possibilities both for good and evil. This we owe to physical science. Again, astronomy is telling us more and more of the vastness and complexity of the boundless universe of which our world is an infinitesimally tiny speck. And we should be very grateful to the scientists for all that they are revealing to us, for it gives us a far wider view of the wonder and majesty of the God who created and brought the universe into existence.

But the tragedy is that our investigation into spiritual laws has lagged and still lags woefully behind our knowledge of natural laws. In a word, dazzled as we are by our increasing awareness of *how* the universe works, we are still pitifully ignorant of *why* it works. We know, so to speak, how to get from King's Cross to Edinburgh, but we are puzzled as to why we do, or the purpose or value of our journey. One reason for this lack of growth in spiritual things is our very pre-occupation with the material side of life. Another is that spiritual laws and values are among the imponderables. They cannot be weighed and measured as can the material things with which physical science deals. You can say "Thy sins be forgiven thee", but, unless you can read a man's heart, you cannot clinically check whether it takes place, whereas you can see with your eyes whether a man rises and walks. The very things on which Divine Healing depends—faith, prayer, the laying on of hands, and unction—are spiritual forces, and though their effects may be seen, of the actual working of them we have far too little knowledge.

As a result we are apt to apply to the cures of spiritual healing the epithet "miraculous". In one sense, of course, they are miraculous. They are the wonderful works of GOD. But they are not violations of law, but rather the application by God of a higher supernatural law. But into the working of these spiritual or supernatural laws there has as yet been little investigation. For instance, take the working of unction or the laying on of hands. "Merely suggestion," some doctors are inclined to say. And no doubt suggestion forms a part of the technique. But is there not something else—the activity of God Himself, the working of His spiritual law? This is very hard to express, but I am sure there is a real point here and it calls for investigation. Of course in matters spiritual, *omnia exeunt in mysterium*. But we should go as far as our finite minds permit. God is the author of all healing, and the *vis medicatrix naturae* is the working of His spirit of life, which is always working to keep our whole person well.

What really is it that prayer, unction and laying on of hands contribute to the healing of a patient? It is clear what the physician or surgeon is doing. He is using material means, drugs or surgery. But many doctors would admit that they are by material means enabling the *vis medicatrix naturae* to operate. As one doctor said of a patient, "I treated him: God healed him." But what of the priest? He claims to be using spiritual means, like prayer. But what does he really do? Is it only a strong form of suggestion, as some doctors imply? Surely the priest's action does two things: (1) it removes the obstacles to the inflow of God's healing power; and (2) it brings the patient into lifegiving touch with God's healing activity.

First, it removes the blocks in the sick person's mind or spirit which close the entry to God's healing. This is abundantly clear in the case of the paralytic whom our Lord healed at Capernaum. What prevented his recovery was the sense of being unforgiven and unforgiveable. So before He did anything

53

else our Lord, reading his inmost heart, said, "Be of good cheer, thy sins are forgiven thee" (Matt. 9: 2). Then at once the paralysing block was removed, and he was able to respond successfully to the action of God's lifegiving spirit.

Secondly, prayer brings the patient into vital touch with Christ. In Christian prayer there is no question of persuading a reluctant God to do something which He does not want to do. For "All that I have is thine", and "He who spared not His own Son but delivered Him up for us all, how shall He not with Him freely give us all things?" (Rom. 8: 32). As far as the willingness and givingness of God goes, the patient is already healed. That is how he is in God's mind. But he is not yet healed on the level of our fact and experience. To be healed he needs faith on his side, and on the side of his friends. Faith is the vital link between God and us, between our mind and God's mind. For, as the Revised Version Margin of Hebrews 11: 1, tells us, faith is "the giving substance to things hoped for". It is the making real on the level of our fact and experience of what is already real in the mind of God. This is the faith of prayer on its affirmative side. Is it not perhaps something of this sort which lies behind our Lord's deeply challenging words in Mark 11: 24, "All things whatsoever ye pray and ask for, believe that ye have received them [i.e. that as far as the willingness of God goes they are yours] and ye shall have them"? And note that this amazing promise is recorded in the earliest Gospel.

The same line of thought might be followed in dealing with unction and laying on of hands. They are not mere suggestion, but sacramental points of contact between Christ and us, the linking point being, as in affirmative prayer, faith.

We have tried to give as positive an answer as possible to some of the many theological and intellectual problems raised by the modern revival of Divine Healing. Shall we end by trying to see what is the purpose of God in all this? Surely God is working for the perfect integration of human personality in harmony with the Divine, so that we come to a Perfect

Man, to the measure of the stature of the fulness of Christ. That is God's purpose, integration in harmony with Himself. That demands a healthy body, a healthy mind, and a healthy spirit. This perfection the Incarnate Christ has displayed, and, however long the road, God will not be content till we attain His goal. For He is our life and our health.

4

THE DAILY ROUND OF SUFFERING AND HEALING

by Dr. Robert A. Lambourne

Dr. Lambourne, M.B., Ch.B., is a native of Birmingham and qualified as a medical practitioner after study in the Medical Faculty of Birmingham University. He was House Physician at the Queen Elizabeth Hospital, Birmingham, and is now in private practice in one of the suburbs of the city. He is particularly interested in the social aspects of sickness, disease and medicine, and is making a special study of the interrelation of religious belief and healing.

All Sickness is Communal in its Origin and Suffering

THE GENERAL PRACTITIONER lives and works, often for a lifetime, in one neighbourhood amongst a living community. Thereby he comes to view the sicknesses of his individual patients as not theirs alone, but as affecting all around them in house, family, street, factory or office. Conversely, he sees these same groups by their merits and deficiencies producing health and sickness in the individuals amongst them. Social medicine is part of the G.P.'s art and tradition. Accordingly the author of this essay has chosen to discuss mainly what might perhaps be decribed as the public health side of the Ministry of Healing.

The patient with a gastric ulcer is not often treated nowadays as if it were a detachable defect, like a tear in his jacket. It is accepted that the ulcer is an expression of his whole personality, and that this same personality affects, and is affected by, his environment. Consequently, enquiry about such matters as tension at work and domestic difficulties is considered essential when taking a case history. Nevertheless, experience in general practice suggests that even today the degree of interdependence of individual and community is seldom appreciated.

The general practitioner by observations taken in his daily work is privileged to gain a knowledge of his patients and their environment which is denied even to social workers and other experts, despite their special training and the hours they devote to social research. These, through lack of personal knowledge of the patient, may fail to ask a vital question, or be misled through cover-up answers to intimate questions. It is true that deep and prolonged association with patients by psychiatrists will uncover all relevant material, but this process is limited in extent because of its prohibitive cost in terms of skilled medical labour. Consequently it tends to be employed only in cases where previous experience has already demonstrated that it is likely to be therapeutic. Then it is that the general practitioner is most favourably placed to observe new symptom complexes in which material, mental and spiritual factors seem to play a strong aetiological role. The frequency of these observations and the multiplicity of diseases, trivial and serious, causes the distinction in his mind between organic and psychosomatic disease to fade and finally disappear. He retains the distinction only for filing and other practical purposes, but regards it as purely arbitrary.

There can be no doubt for him that in all disease, mind, body, and spirit are concerned. If spiritual factors are studied as if they occurred apart from mind and body—which they never do—then we can say that in any disease which a person suffers spiritual factors play their part whether that part be a predominant or a small loading factor like the proverbial straw that broke the camel's back.

It follows from demonstrations of psychosomatic disease that if amongst man's nature there is an implanted need to worship

God, then denial of that need must have effects which may be measurable in the physical body. But perhaps insufficient attention has been given by those interested in Divine Healing to the corresponding implications of the teachings of social or group psychology on the interaction of the individual mind and the community. If the beliefs and lives of the group profoundly influence that of the individual, then new possibilities emerge. The case history of our gastric-ulcer patient must be further extended to incorporate not only the physical and mental health of his environment but also the spiritual state of his community. A public health department of Divine Healing is required to study those spiritual factors in communities which are tonic or healing.

Included in our case history of a gastric-ulcer patient may be the following: He is tense and anxious and inclined to be aggressive. This seems to be connected with a feeling of guilt about a woman he is associating with at work. Part of the responsibility for this misconduct lies with his wife who is cold and bothers him with her social ambitions. She had an unhappy childhood—poverty and too many children. This poverty is a social sin for which we are responsible. What we have done or failed to do, for physical, psychological and spiritual reasons, is part of our patient's case history. We bear joint responsibility with him for some aetiological factors in his disease.

This fact, that in realms of sickness and healing we are "many members but one body", seems to be more fully appreciated by those whose approach to sickness is physical or psychological than by those whose main interest is in the spiritual factors concerned. A correction of a too individualistic approach in Divine Healing is required for it to be firmly based.

All Disease is a Challenging Situation to Individual and Community Alike

The realisation in the scientific field of the degree to which the mind and body are an interdependent unity has encouraged those interested in Divine Healing to adapt these concepts and speak of the "wholeness" of man. Some then assert that such "wholeness" is God's will for all of us, and that if we perfectly trust in Him He will give it us. They hasten to qualify this, as indeed they must, for the sufferings of Christ and the ailments of the saints throw grave doubts upon it. These difficulties become more complex the deeper we study them, and reflection suggests that the root cause is that for our modern mind the word "wholeness" has implications which are un-Biblical. Perfect "wholeness" is associated in our mind with perfect forms like Chinese vases, Greek sculpture and efficien machinery. But Biblical "wholeness" is not one of "form" but one of "action". Sin is not a departure from a formalised perfection, it is wrong action. Perfection lies in perfect attitude towards God, not in a man's perfect wholeness of form. Christ on the Cross is perfect in obedience and love, not in form, for the gaping flesh and the flowing blood deny Him perfection of form.

Because of the inescapable associations for our contemporary mind, of "form" with the word "wholeness", we should give it honourable burial and look for another which is associated with action and direction. We shall choose "response". It is God's will for us, we may say, to respond perfectly to all situations including disease and lack of wholeness. This terminology has the great advantage for the theology of the Ministry of Healing that it does not make distinctions between disease and other situations, both good and bad, which confront us. Disease, like war, sin, injustice and other adversity, confronts individual and community with a call from God to respond to it perfectly. The importance of choosing a terminology in the Ministry of Healing which does not put disease apart from other human crisis situations is that it stifles that curse associated with Divine Healing, the belief that prayer and practical action are irreconcilable. We assert that all situations, including disease, require both prayer and other practical actions. A row with the wife calls for prayer and giving up night work with its lucrative pay. A husband's coronary thrombosis calls for prayer and a change to light work and less money.

"Response" also has the advantage of fitting the modern concept of One World in which all men and women are joined in never-ending responses and interactions of mind, body, and spirit. The response to disease, as modern civilisations affirm by their national health schemes, is required not just from the individual with the disease but from all men. Not even national boundaries limit the responsibility, so U.N.N.R.A. and medical missionaries must cross these boundaries. The perfect response cannot be given to disease situations by individuals alone but only within a community which responds with them. Thus an alcoholic is facing a critical disease situation, but the critical situation is not his alone, but all men's and his response must be with other men. No better example of this can be cited than Alcoholics Anonymous where a society reaches out to assist the sufferer, because they feel that his suffering is theirs. And the sufferer turns towards it because he feels that his disease, sin and shame is accepted and shared. Here is a prototype of a healing society which is always moving outwards to assist fellow sufferers and drawing them into a fellowship where they can find faith, hope and love. How shall we describe the quality which makes such a healing community and how shall we establish such a community?

The Ultimate Judgement of our Response to Disease is Its Quality and not Its Success

The answer to this question will be left to the next two sections whilst we defend this statement. It is often suggested by enthusiasts for Divine Healing that only our lack of faith and dependence upon God stands between us and healing. This leads to grave problems for sick and faithful people and for those who witness their suffering. In view of this, and the scriptural assertion that Christ was both perfect and suffered, we do better to teach only that God requires of us to respond to disease according to His will, and judges us by the quality of our response to our own and other people's suffering.

This is not a hopeless message, but the contrary, for, as we shall argue later, the correct response releases great healing powers both in the individual and the community. Moreover, in our last section on suffering we shall argue that God uses our obedient response to disease by producing good out of evil, though the goodness is not necessarily that of cure. If we believe that God rewards faith and prayer in the face of disease by removing that disease in proportion, then we are doomed to despair, for death always has the last laugh. If we believe that God uses the quality of our response to disease to create good out of evil and further His plans, then we are raised to hope, for by a good response to all disease we are partners with Him even at the hour of death.

It should be reiterated, lest it is not already quite clear, that the perfect response of individual and community to any evil includes a desire to remove the evil completely, to eradicate all suffering. This is its normal and proper tactical objective for the daily round and common task. But as God judges us by the quality of our response and not by its tactical success, so we must not judge it *ultimately* by its tactical success but by its quality and its use in God's strategy.

A patient with an industrial injury may by his efforts and those of his family, his doctor and various ancillary services be restored to normal health. Yet at the end of it he may be harder, more bitter, more selfish and grasping than before, cursing God and society which has allowed this to happen to him. He will bring sorrow to many in his family and friends. Alternatively, the same patient may, despite everybody's efforts, remain seriously crippled. Yet he may be a kinder, more thoughtful, humbler, more loving man, with great powers of helping and lifting others in his circle. The first case is a tactical success and a strategical failure; the second quite the opposite. It is because of this kind of experience, not to mention our friends who include both saintly sufferers and healthy villains, that we see no ultimate criterion of the response to disease but its quality.

THE PERFECT QUALITY OF RESPONSE TO DISEASE IS ACTIVITY POWERED BY LOVE, AND THIS LOVE HAS HEALING POWER

Others in this symposium describe how the faith, hope and love of a sick man can assist him in his healing. We need, therefore, only briefly touch on a few points.

The love we write of is not a sentimental substitute for action but an active relationship between men, women and God. It is shown to perfection in the life of Jesus Christ. It includes compassion, suffering, justice, prayer, surgery, and all the range of man's Godward activities. It is seen every day when men and women meet poverty, sickness, war and other situations with courage, patience and self-sacrifice. It is demonstrated by those who simultaneously fight desperately for health and suffer patiently; men and women who declare in their lives what St. Paul wrote to the Corinthians, "Love beareth all things, believeth all things, hopeth all things, endureth all things" (1 Cor. 13: 7). He might have also written "Hateth all disease, endureth all disease, overcometh all disease" but *not* "cureth all disease". Where will such love be found and how can it help us?

HEALING LOVE IS FOUND IN THE FELLOWSHIP OF COMMUNITIES

Love is nurtured and expressed in personal relationships, in the give-and-take of family life and other social groups. Child psychologists have convincingly demonstrated how parental love is essential for a child's natural and full development. The child grows to maturity in the receiving and giving of love. What is true of the child is true also of the adult. We grow from spiritual childhood to maturity by giving and receiving love, and this can only take place within a community of two or more. To belong to a community, whether it be friends, family, neighbourhood, club, factory, church, or office, is to be exposed to hygienic and healing forces proportionate to the love which binds that community.

Most doctors can recall examples of patients whose diseases have been healed by a community. The community which has been given most attention is the family where the child is nurtured in hygienic and healing love. But of course the parents in the family are exposed to the same forces. So we see in general practice just as many patients healed by becoming members of other kinds of communities, such as Churches, Mothers' Union, Darby and Joan clubs, to mention a few of the more prominent.

There is no disease more frequently prevented and cured by community than the commonest of all diseases, the anxiety state. Fellowship gives a feeling of security, and troubles are lightened by sharing. If the particular community is fortunate enough to be relatively free from the restlessness and anxiety that besets modern society, then the fellowship of that community will be correspondingly healing.

It is noticeable how many patients find health when they join a sectarian church. This perhaps is because whatever the oddities of its theology, it is a group which has the two great healing virtues of a sense of corporateness and a conviction of election. The members believe themselves to be one with another and this is healing. They are convinced that they are chosen of God and destined to salvation, so that worldly anxieties are swallowed up in other-worldly confidence. It is unfortunate that, whilst these groups bring health to many, their oddities of theology often cast aspersions on orthodox medicine and thus expose their members to unnecessary suffering and death. Sound theology is as important as sound medicine in the Ministry of Healing!

Where shall we find a fellowship which reacts to disease with healing love? The founding and development of such a community is described in the New Testament.

63

LOCAL CHRISTIAN FELLOWSHIP MUST PROVIDE THE BASIS OF THE MINISTRY OF HEALING

We have spoken of fellowship in communities as hygienic and healing. We have affirmed that these powers are by virtue of the love which binds them. This answers those who speak as if all communities were equally healing, ranging from a pack of thieves cemented by mutual self-interest to a dedicated group cemented by self-sacrificing love. The quality of the community is vital to its healing powers, and the measure of its quality is love. In the early chapters of the Acts of the Apostles we see the founding of a fellowship which is the model of the healing community. This must sound unlikely not only to non-Christians but to many Christians for whom the Church is just another mutually self-regarding club. We can only refer them to the Acts (e.g. 4: 33–35) and also to the writings and efforts of those who are now grappling with the contemporary problem.

The local Christian fellowship gathered around a home, street, factory or office, and based on the local church with its sacraments available through its ministry, both receives strength together and faces its problems together. One man's unemployment is its corporate concern. A second man's sickness is their predicament. A third man's sin is their crisis. Guided by trained hands and by their own experience they become spiritually mature. And it is within such a spiritually mature group that the Ministry of Healing can safely and profitably operate.

Without the local fellowship the Ministry of Healing is like a specialist medical service which has no hospitals and no public health clinics. The local fellowship provides not only a healing and hygienic force which can percolate its neighbourhood and reduce disease, but also it provides a follow-up treatment for the specialist's patients. The local minister or doctor may be able to bring together his patients and the church in his own street and be sure that the patient will be supported by that group.

Not only is the local fellowship which has gained spiritual maturity essential to make the Ministry of Healing more fruitful. It is essential in order to make it safe! For it is a training ground in the Christian reaction to adversity which enables sick men and women to keep their theological balance when they look for Divine Healing. In no other field does heresy so quickly produce material disaster. Sick people and their relatives fly from one extreme to the other. Having always put their entire trust in scientific medicine, they suddenly come to believe it is more holy to pray than to operate. In other challenging situations they will practise both prayer and scientific action, fighting the tempest by both prayer and manning the pumps. But in sickness they feel guilty about one if they do another, as if science and Christ were two gods jealous of each other. Yet Christianity affirms that Christ was God incarnate "in whom are hid all the treasures of wisdom and knowledge" (Col. 2: 3). These theological distinctions are difficult for those untrained in them, but a balance which intellectually is hard to hold can be gained by all in the practice of the local fellowship. Here by facing together all the difficulties of daily life with acts both of prayer and science they come to learn a pattern of response which stands by them when personal sickness crises confront them.

THE MINISTRY OF SUFFERING COMPLETES THE MINISTRY OF HEALING

Man's response to suffering must include not only the effort to eradicate it but a willingness to suffer it. A theology of health must be balanced by a theology of suffering. Otherwise, faithful Christian people called to face disease by placing themselves in the hands of God who wills to heal them will be discouraged and shamed by their continuing suffering. And because death comes to all, all will be discouraged and shamed. But the Gospel tells us clearly that if a perfect response is made by man (i.e. Christ) to suffering (i.e. His Passion), then God will

c   65

join in that perfect response not to eradicate that suffering (the Crucifixion is not averted) but to work His plan for man's salvation (the Atonement). So God has written at the centre of history the principle that out of suffering He can, with man's free co-operation, produce salvation. Suffering is evil still, but it can be made to work a good purpose. It is no longer senseless.

This bald and unacceptable truth (a truth which rings an alarm bell in the minds of progressives who have strong folk-memories of its use to defend social injustice) is supported by others than theological fanatics. Educationalists base much of their theory and practice upon it, asserting that groups of children encouraged to surmount difficulties together gain in personal maturity and corporate sense. Historians trace the rise and fall of civilisation to man's response to adversity. Much of Greek tragedy is written on this theme. Biologists trace connections between the challenge of environment and selection and development of more complex organisms. The truth is written in Nature as well as Creed.

This truth is not an easy one for the sick man in the middle of his suffering. Neither is it easily affirmed by those who enjoy embarrassingly good health. But some are called by God to a state of suffering in which they qualify to witness to the truth. They have a vocation of suffering which qualifies them for the Ministry of Suffering. Others qualify by devoting their lives to remove suffering. The first group includes those wonderful men and women who uplift us by their example in terrible sickness and pain. The second group can include us all. The family doctor especially, by his vigorous and conscientious efforts to relieve suffering at the expense of his own convenience, may satisfy himself and others that he takes suffering seriously. He may then speak of God's Ministry of Suffering.

This belief in the Ministry of Suffering as well as the Ministry of Healing enables the doctor to speak words of comfort and encouragement to all sorts and conditions of men, not just to those for whom a cure can be foreseen. By it the elderly bed-ridden patient can be comforted in the face of her feeling that she is "just a nuisance, Doctor". She can be assured that by her godly suffering she can strengthen the doctor, family and neighbours. The belief brings strength to the sick child's parents and comfort to the bereaved. It provides a sound basis for doctor-patient relationship. Every disease is not just another round of a battle in which disease and death always finally defeat both doctor and patient. Every sickness situation is an opportunity to doctor and patient to be joint partners with God in His great plan, for in Jesus Christ He has shown that if they will work with Him, He will use that sickness-situation for their own and all men's salvation. He will give them the power to overcome all things, even the last enemy, Death.

✠

PART II

THE ANSWER

✠

5

BACK FROM THE VALLEY

by Hugh Redwood, O.B.E.

Hugh Redwood's book, Residue of Days,[1] *from which the following contribution is taken, by permission, was written as "a confession of faith" in his seventy-fifth year. A year earlier he had heard the doctors pronounce what amounted to a death sentence, and had been shown the evidence on which it was based. But instead, and without the severe operation he had been urged to undergo, he found himself given a renewed lease of life and restored to normal health.*

As a journalist, he knew that this could have been made a front-page story. But to treat it as such would, in his view, have been wholly wrong, and both he and his publishers were at great pains to guard against the sensationalising of the facts. Because their importance is incidental rather than primal they were set out in the latter half of the book, which treats of the grounds on which he holds the beliefs set forth in its earlier chapters, and readers of the present volume are asked to consider them in this light.

JUST WITHIN the churchyard gateway in the Devon village of Uplowman there is a grave-stone bearing the name

Hugh Redwood

It is that of my grandfather, sometime village blacksmith of this, my father's birthplace. I never saw him, for he died before I was born, and when I first set eyes on his grave, in the summer of 1954, I had only once previously been in

[1] *Residue of Days,* published by Hodder and Stoughton, London.

Uplowman. Even then, I stayed less than an hour, talking to two distant cousins, whom I found in charge at the post-office.

But at the sight of that stone a strange thing happened. I was seized with a sense of homecoming. It was as if something within me had wakened to the knowledge that it belonged here. I felt a great desire to come again, to come and preach in the parish church, where my father had been one of the ringers. In the spring of the following year the wish was gratified. I preached at the Sunday morning service, and in the afternoon the rector, who had conducted it, wrote me the kindest of letters:

"I have a strong feeling," he said, "that this morning was God's moment, and that there was an underlying purpose for it, in addition to the personal joy it brought you in His goodness. It so happens that I am sharing with my people, in a series of Eastertide sermons, some reflections on the 23rd Psalm. Tonight I shall be speaking on the verse 'Yea, though I walk through the valley of the shadow of death . . .' with the strongest possible emphasis on the presence of God through all the changing scenes of life. You know that the assurance of that presence is the greatest treasure we can possess, and that it is the only comfort when we come to the last valley of all. I pray that He will ever be with you, and lead you home. It is His presence that makes Heaven 'home', because He is love."

I have quoted his letter because it now takes place in my mind as part of the pattern of things, in which the leading motif is a blend of home-coming and homeward-leading. It recurred often that year, pointing backward and forward, both. Thus there were days when I lived again in the Bristol of my boyhood; and if you have a fancy for coincidences (as I hope you have, because there will be more of them before this chapter is finished), try to work out the chances against such a coincidence as this one, which took me home in the most literal sense.

At lunch in Croydon I got into conversation with a man to whom I had been introduced as a fellow-Bristolian, that is to say a fellow-citizen of no mean city which, while it may not be a "great wen" like London, has nevertheless a population of nearly half a million. How unlikely that home, for this man, should be the identical house in which I had lived as a child, undamaged in Bristol's fierce blitz and changed only by the addition of a bathroom. But so it was: I went to see him there soon afterwards, and the room in which we sat and yarned was familiar and friendly despite the lapse of wellnigh seventy years.

On another Bristol occasion I spoke to the boys of the Cathedral School, from which I had launched straight into journalism. And somewhere on the road to Gloucester, I met a playmate of days long ago who had lately emerged from the dark valley and told me of God's upholding there.

Surely, these too were God's moments; assurances of His underlying purpose. His presence through all life's changing scenes. "The greatest treasure we can possess . . . the only comfort when we come to the last valley of all." The words of a good man journeyed with me.

II

In June 1956 I made a short stay in the West Country, fulfilling a couple of speaking engagements and visiting friends old and new. At the end of the month I came home, a little tired but otherwise feeling quite fit, and thanking God for a time of special happiness, in which the homecoming note had again been struck. I had met one who had been on my prayer list for years, and for whom during that period of tragedy, the most diligent search had proved unavailing. Now, by the grace of God, she was home again. We had been planning for the future, and she had said that if opportunity came she would read the

Bible for me in one of my meetings. Then on the run back to London I had spent an hour, packed with memories, in the company of a friend whom I had last seen fifty years previously, when she and her husband were sailing for China.

It was all good to look back upon, but now there was work in plenty to be done; speaking engagements, a Sunday night "epilogue" on B.B.C. Television, and the fearsome mass of correspondence which accumulates when a man retires and becomes, of necessity, his own private secretary, unpaid. I kept the engagements, but the tiredness increased, and with it now came something different, until negative turned to positive and "not feeling well" became "feeling ill".

I said nothing about it, at first, to my wife, for she herself was not well and I did not want her to worry, but with the worsening of the symptoms came increasing suspicion of their origin and just for a little while I knew a dread which brought me near to panic. In the small hours of the morning I awoke in its grip and could do nothing to break it. Even thought seemed paralysed and unable to collect the words of prayer. How long this went on I cannot say: I know only that it seemed a very long time and that it ended all at once. With the clock striking five, I dropped peacefully back into sleep, and peace stayed on when I woke.

The date was July 19, and I was to have occasion to note it in my diary. That morning a man in Monmouthshire wrote to me. We had met, I think, only once, and exchanged less than a dozen letters in as many years; but I knew him for a good man and a praying man, and now from him came a note, brief and urgent, to ask if all was well. "I woke very early this morning," it ran, "not to sleep again until you came into my mind, at five o'clock, when I prayed and had rest. I don't know the reason." No, he didn't and couldn't know the reason then, any more than we can when the prompting comes, without obvious cause, to pray for some particular person. Nor could I then have told him the reason as clearly as I see it now. I could and did tell him that he was God's messenger to me; but later I knew that he met me at the entrance to the Valley of the Shadow, to let me know I should not be alone.

In a day or two more, my wife became anxious and urged me to call in the doctor. Having little doubt what he would say, I played for time on her account, and told her that if I felt no better I would ring him up in the morning. That was July 23, and in the afternoon, without being sent for, he called. Perhaps I should put it differently. He too was a praying man, but this thing might have a perfectly ordinary explanation. "I wonder who asked you to come," I said. "Was it my wife, or was it the Almighty?" to which he replied, "Well, it wasn't your wife."

He came, in fact, because, in his surgery, he had suddenly felt that he must. It is a great thing to have a man like that for a doctor; a Christian to whom one can talk as such. He advised an X-ray examination, and promised to tell me the result in plain English, though it was clear that he was thinking in terms of hospital and an operation. I knew, after that, what I had to do next.

In my quiet hour, the following morning, I made an unreserved recommittal of myself to Christ:

> "The great Physician now is near,
> The sympathising Jesus."

I felt it was true, and I put myself, *for life or death*, entirely in His hands. We did not then know the full seriousness of affairs, but He gave me deliverance from fear from that moment. It is not a boast, but a deeply humble and grateful testimony.

Can we talk of the Lord confirming an agreement in writing? Consider this. Within an hour or two of my recommittal, a friend then living in the New Forest was writing a letter which began with these words:

> "Good morning, dear brother. You are able to greet this day with joy, I feel sure, knowing the Hand of God is upon

75

you. You have today, 6.55 a.m., gripped afresh the nail-
pierced Hand, and received new strength and vigour."

Don't ask me how she knew, even to the actual time. I cannot
explain; I can only record, and wonder. I learned to value her
prayers when she was a slum officer in the Salvation Army, and
there were times even then when she seemed to have channels
of knowledge which passed my comprehension. I had mentioned in a letter to her that I had not been feeling well, and I
had asked for her remembrance in prayer; but here she was,
abreast of a transaction which I was thinking of as a secret,
shared only by Him with whom it was completed; and reading
her words I knew the peace which is greater than man's understanding.

The X-ray examination duly took place and was followed
by an interview with a hospital surgeon who spoke of having
me in for observation and treatment. He mentioned an
intestinal obstruction, but did not specify its nature. In fact,
as a written statement by my own doctor sets forth, in the
plain language which he had promised, the X-ray examination
revealed "a carcinoma (cancer) of the pelvirectal junction,
about the size of a small hen's egg, pressing on the bowel".
Without telling me this, in so many words, the doctor made it
plain to me that, for fuller examination and treatment, I ought
to enter hospital without avoidable delay; and this I did as soon
as I had taken such steps as I could to leave my affairs in order.
There was no need of detailed information: I knew the truth
already, and the only thing which came as a surprise was that
all dread of it had departed. This again is written in no boastful
spirit: for the rest of my days, few or many, the thought of what
happened will keep me in awe.

It seems to me now that I went into hospital not to be healed,
but to learn. The very first thing I learned was that, although
I had never seen him before, the man in the next bed to mine
was one with whom I had a close link. He was the chief proof-
reader of a magazine to which I have long been a regular

contributor, and we were friends within an hour. Nor was that all: one of the printers was in the same ward. It meant a lot to all three of us: one wonders how it came about.

The day came when I woke with crashings in my ears, flashes of searing light in my eyes, and a general feeling of having been split asunder. I ran my hands hurriedly over my body, and was puzzled to find it all in one piece and, so far as I could judge, undamaged. No wound, no bandages or strappings, no particular pain: only a tempest of noise in which I began to distinguish three voices, all speaking at once and incoherently. Then bodies attached themselves to two of the voices, and I dimly perceived, leaning over at unnatural angles, a nurse and a fellow-patient. The third party remained a voice, a loud and foolish voice, the voice of a loud and very foolish person, for whom I felt a violent dislike until I found that the voice was my own. The operation was over.

It had not been a major one; only a sigmoidoscopy, a surgical survey. With what result? I could not at that time persuade them to say. But a week later they sent me again to the X-ray department, and this time the examination was a much longer one. That evening they explained to me why they felt I should have a second operation, and what it might very well involve. Their language, though guarded, was grave, but in some queer way I found myself listening to it as if it concerned someone else. The operation of which they talked sounded almost incredible, but if I shrank from some of the details it was not because I could see myself on the operating table. The truth was that I couldn't. What I could see, and very distinctly, was that a man of my age, even if he survived such an operation, would no longer be fit for the kind of work which, to me, was life itself. He would inevitably become a burden to his loved ones as well as himself, and the two people dearest to me were burdened enough already.

The imperative need to operate, as seen by the surgeons, is revealed in my own doctor's statement from which I have previously quoted. In twenty days the carcinoma had roughly doubled its size, which was now that of a small orange. It was causing an increased degree of obstruction, and it was still growing. If there was to be an operation, it must be performed in not more than a week, and it would take four days to prepare me for it. I was a free agent: I had the right to choose; but I must decide quickly. It was Monday evening: I promised to give my decision by Wednesday.

It was made, in fact, next morning, in a quiet corner of the hospital grounds. This was a matter of life and death; by God's help I must make no mistakes. I was committed to Him, and the feeling was strong within me that I should not agree to the operation; but I wanted to be sure that this feeling was genuine conviction, and not just funk masquerading as faith. So, acting on the advice of the hymn, I "took it to the Lord in prayer", and the help I asked for came flooding in. I was in the Valley, but my Shepherd was with me. . . . I could give my decision and fear no evil.

A message sent through my wife brought our doctor to the hospital, and he and I then went into conference with the surgeon who had spoken to me on the previous day. On this occasion, by common consent, the plainest speech was used by us all. The X-ray films were produced and interpreted to me, though indeed they, too, spoke plainly enough. There was no denying what they revealed, and the surgeon, repeating and emphasising his advice in favour of an operation, asked if I had given any more thought to it.

"Yes," I said. "I have both thought about it and prayed about it, and now I have made my decision. I hope you will bear with me while I explain it. I have definitely decided against the operation."

"You must forgive me," he interrupted, "for telling you that, in my opinion, you are making a very grave mistake."

He needed no forgiveness from me. I was perfectly sure, and I said so, that were I in his place, I should be saying what he had just said. What I asked him to believe was that I was not being stubborn, ungrateful, or unco-operative; that I accepted the validity of the grounds on which his advice was based, but that there were grounds for my decision which to me were equally valid. He gave me the most patient and sympathetic of hearings while I spoke of my committal to Christ; but he asked if I felt that such action necessarily excluded medical or surgical help; to which I replied with a very firm negative, believing that doctors and surgeons, as surely as journalists and other folk, should dedicate their work to God.

The considerations which had influenced me were these:

1. I was sure that Christ *could* heal me.

2. I was equally sure that my work for Him was not yet done.

3. It was a reasonable assumption, in view of my age, that the end of my course could not be far distant; and the nature of my committal to Him made me confident that He would enable me to finish it, whether by a complete healing or by a sufficient extension of life and strength.

4. The proposed operation, on the other hand, was so severe that while it might prolong my life—if it did not kill me outright—it would rule out any possibility of resuming the special work to which I felt called.

When I had stated my case, my doctor, at a nod from the surgeon, took up the X-ray film and the parable.

"I am going to speak now solely as a doctor," he said, "and because I am your doctor, it is my duty to tell you that, if you do not have this operation, I shall not expect to find you alive at Christmas."

Medically speaking, it was a death sentence, and it surprises me, even now, to remember how it affected me; for what I felt was nothing like fear, but rather a sense of excitement, as of one who grasps the measure of that which God is about to do for him. Just now, when I was casting about for words to describe it, I thought of the children of Israel, caught in Pharaoh's death-trap beside the Red Sea. So, perhaps, may some of them have felt, when they heard the ringing voice of Moses and understood what he was saying to them: "Fear ye not, stand still, and see the salvation of the Lord, which He will show you today."

And then my good doctor, having said what he felt it his duty to say, openly ranged himself on my side and declared that, as a Christian, he believed I was doing the right thing. "You must try to understand this man as I do," he said to the surgeon. "He lives in two worlds at once, and I think he feels at home in both, so that the question of life or death doesn't weigh with him overmuch as a personal matter. It's a case for his conscience, and, knowing the facts, I don't see how he could reach any other decision."

After that, things happened swiftly. In the friendliest atmosphere all round, I signed the form of self-discharge and went happily home to my wife in the doctor's car.

It was August 21: Christmas was only four months off. But from that moment life steadily returned to normal. In a week I was back on a healthy man's diet: in a month I was speaking in public again. And there is a note in my diary to remind me that on September 18 I ordered my Christmas cards and bought my new year's engagement-book.

III

When Christmas came, my doctor, finding me not only alive but well, wrote at my request the statement from which I have already quoted. Long before then he verbally confessed to the very grave doubt he had felt of my life being saved, even by drastic surgery. But read now his own version of the incidents just set down and what followed them.

"The hospital surgeon and I informed Mr. Redwood that an operation was imperative to save his life. Without it, he would again develop acute obstruction within a matter of days, and would be likely to die within a very short time. If he was prepared to undergo the operation, it might be possible to prolong his life by a few months or even from one to two years.

"Mr. Redwood, however, had come to the little conference room which we had borrowed from the Ward Sister, after a time of prayer alone in the hospital grounds; and he calmly informed us that he would not be having the operation, as he felt he had had a clear leading in the matter. I knew then that it would be useless and wrong to try to persuade him otherwise. . . . It was again stressed to him (by the surgeon) that if the operation were not performed, he would have to return within a few days for an emergency operation. But he stood firm, and I smiled as I listened to him, for he and I now seemed to be talking the same language, although in all my medical experience I had never known such an awe-inspiring situation. I suggested that he should pack up his things, and that I should take him home, which I did.

"I contacted as many devout Christians as I could in the next few days, asking their prayers for him. I called regularly to see him in the following weeks, somewhat faithlessly at first, and half expecting him to report a downward trend or a reappearance of the symptoms, but on each occasion he reported improvement.

"And now it is Christmas. For the first time in my life I have witnessed, in this healing, a Divine miracle. In fact, I feel almost as if I had been face to face with the Creator Himself."

No doctor uses the word "healing" lightly, especially in such a connection. I accept it here because I know what he meant by it. Years ago I became acquainted with a woman who had been instantaneously and permanently healed of an external cancer at the base of her throat. She and her husband were retired officers of the Salvation Army, and her husband vouched for the truth of her story, which was that the cancer suddenly *went* during a meeting addressed by a prominent Salvationist who was then practising a healing ministry. She did not feel this astonishing thing happen; all of which she was conscious was a spiritual exaltation and a lifting-up of her faith towards Christ: but putting her hand instinctively to the place where the cancer had been, she discovered that it was no longer there. Fantastic though it may sound, it had completely vanished. To the best of my belief, there was no recurrence. I met her frequently over a period of several years before the Second World War, and her health always appeared to be perfect.

Now what happened in my own case was something quite different from that, and I am glad of it. With my decision to decline the operation and leave the issue in Christ's hands, there came, not an immediate disappearance of the trouble, but the instant beginning of an improvement, unmistakable but gradual. There was no more pain, and only minor and diminishing discomfort, but I felt from the first that henceforward I must live a day at a time; that "healing", in the sense of immediate restoration, mattered much less than living sufficiently long and fully. Then it was that I came across the hymn of Charles Wesley's from which the title of my book has been taken. Strangely, I had never before noticed it, but now, reading its two short verses during my quiet hour one morning, I saw how exactly it fitted my case, and made it a pledge for daily renewal:

> Lord, in the strength of grace,
> With a glad heart, and free,
> Myself, my residue of days
> I consecrate to Thee.
>
> Thy ransomed servant, I
> Restore to Thee Thy own,
> And, from this moment, live or die
> To serve my God alone.

Morning by morning, my prayer since then has been for grace in the measure of the day's need; multiform grace, compounded of faith and trust, assurance and acceptance, strength and perseverance; and I am in a position now to see that living thus, in a dependence on God acknowledged afresh at the start of each day, has been an experience and an education beyond anything likely to have resulted from a cure complete in a moment. The thorn in the flesh and grace sufficient are closely related, as Paul knew well. And God has His own ways of acknowledging and assisting a trust in which our faith must consciously outstep our human reason. Thus, through a praying friend, as I have related, I received an acknowledgment of my committal; and again when, trusting in him, I came home from hospital, there reached me a word to make trust easier.

The publishers, during my absence, had sent me a book compiled from the writings of the late Dr. Rebecca Beard,[1] an American physician whose deep faith in God, strengthened by experience in her profession, led her, with her husband, to concentrate on psychosomatics and establish a centre for spiritual therapy. Without having even glanced at its contents, I brought it to the breakfast table the day following my return, expecting to find some passage in it suitable for our morning devotions. It opened, as I picked it up, at a page on which I read five words: "*the doctors advised a colostomy*". I exclaimed aloud, for this was the operation which the doctors had urged on me; and when my wife asked what I had found, I answered by reading it to her.

To Merrybrook, Dr. Beard's healing centre, there came a business man, "Sam", deeply anxious about his friend "Jimmy", who was grievously sick and afraid. It was Jimmy who had been advised to have the operation, but because of his fears it was deferred, in spite of pain and haemorrhages; and meanwhile Sam went on vacation, sought out Dr. Beard, and with her help gave himself up to prayer for his friend. "In every meeting," he afterwards said, "I held that boy in my love and gave him to God in love." And presently, over the telephone, Jimmy told him what had resulted. He went to the

---

[1] *Everyman's Adventure*, by Rebecca Beard (Arthur James Ltd., Evesham).

doctor for a routine check, and the doctor observed that he was looking better. Jimmy replied that he was feeling fine, and that all pain and discomfort had left him. "So the doctor made an examination, and found that the condition that had been present before had now strangely disappeared. The operation was no longer needed."

I cannot think it was merely chance which brought me that story, *at that moment*.

IV

Over a year has now gone by,[2] over a year of my extended lease, since I came out of hospital, and surely the time has passed more swiftly than ever it passed before. If it seems to have done so it is, I suppose, because living a day at a time one is eager to get each day's full measure and does not keep looking at the clock, or even the calendar. I feel that I have had heavenly measure, "pressed down and shaken together and running over".

The strength of grace has been a fact of daily experience. Poured out through many channels, it has so constantly sufficed to meet the day's need, however great or unexpected, that any concern regarding the morrow's has been quite out of the question. I think of what Christ has been to me, I press down His blessings and shake them together, and my heart runs over in gratitude for that to which they add up: a closer walk with God along a road which is ever homeward.

"I pray that He will ever be with you, and lead you home." That benison from a Devon rectory calls back to mind the hymn my mother loved best. It is "like bells at evening pealing" and "the music of the Gospel" is in it to bring me on my way. And with it there chimes what my doctor said about living in two worlds at once and feeling at home in both. I often think of that, not only because it echoes my thoughts concerning God's primary purpose for man, but because of the meaning it has for Christians generally. It is a powerful antidote to fear.

[2] This was written in September 1957.

If, accepting that more abundant life which Jesus offers to all of us, we really can feel at home in both worlds, and communicate that feeling to others, there isn't much to be afraid of. After all, it is rather like the two addresses that most of us have, a home address and a business address. The everyday world is our business address, and our business is, or should be, our Father's business. Who's afraid of going home, when the day's work's done?

6

A NEW OPPORTUNITY BEFORE THE CHURCH

by THE REV. CANON E. N. DUCKER

Canon Ducker's ministry has been exercised mostly in the Midlands. He was Vicar of Langley Mill from 1934 to 1938, and has been Vicar of St. Margaret's, Leicester, since 1938. Having been interested for many years in Pastoral Psychology, he founded, with the co-operation of other clergy, the St. Margaret's Clinic for Pastoral Psychology; although many of his colleagues have moved from Leicester he continues the work of the Clinic although hampered by shortage of staff and the many calls that are made on a parish priest.

SOME YEARS ago a group of clergy, with diocesan sanction, formed at St. Margaret's Vicarage, Leicester, what they called, for lack of a better name, The St. Margaret's Clinic for Pastoral Psychology. Most of the members of the team had been practising psychotherapy for many years. The venture brought forth an unceasing supply of persons seeking help, and before long we found ourselves with a waiting list two years long. Unfortunately for some years now I have been working alone, the other members of the team having moved to distant parts of the country, where they are continuing the work.

I will begin by saying something about my methods of treatment, and the various factors which play their part in this healing work. First, I would stress the unique value of the clerical collar and the vicarage as the centre for the work. It is widely believed by many Christian people that most psychiatrists are not professed Christians and that not a few of them are opposed to religion. These people feel that by coming to the vicarage their faith will not be jeopardised, and further they associate with the Church the sympathy and healing love of her Lord. In the case of religiously-minded people this gives a flying start to the treatment and goes a long way towards winning the co-operation of the sick person without which the treatment will fail; but even if people are not definitely religious I think I am right in assuming that they regard the clergyman as a benevolent and sympathetic person. Besides this, most people are excessively concerned with guilt, although much of it may be unconscious; there is a disquiet, to say the least. There are some clergymen who doubtless would only add to this disquiet by their fiery denunciations of sin, and it is unlikely that the guilty person would turn to them for ease of mind; however, there are others who by their understanding spirit will draw people to them, and to such people the guilt-laden souls will turn. Thus the clerical psychotherapists are trusted, and by virtue of their office they have advantages over most people working in this field.

Working in the name of Jesus Christ, I never employ any kind of religious test before accepting a person for treatment; it is sufficient to know that one is able to assist some stricken souls and maybe help to bring new life to them. I have found almost without exception that a person's neurosis sooner or later, under treatment, compels him to face a spiritual issue; in fact the repression of religion and morality is often the root cause of a neurosis and therefore these must be revived before a cure can be effected.

A group of ladies meet to pray for the work of St. Margaret's Clinic, holding before God in prayer persons who during their treatment are in special need.

It is always stressed in the early stages of treatment that the healing work is of the Spirit, who is there in the mysterious depths of the mind of everyman, and that the sufferer must co-operate with God. Fr. Victor White has suggested that the therapist's work is to be likened to that of a midwife who assists only at the birth of the new life. The therapist does not heal. When the new life begins to appear the sick person feels new power and an exhilaration which unless it is checked is beset with peril to life. The pride of Icarus may lead to a disastrous fall. It is when we say "*My power and the might of mine own hand hath gotten me this healing*" (cf. Deut. 8:17), that we are actually most in danger. Now, happily, the Christian therapist can meet this danger by giving a reminder that all good things come from God, who works dynamically in the depths of the mind.

In addition to the spiritual framework with its creative influences within which the majority of people coming to me are included, I make full use of the findings of Freud, Adler, Jung and many others who have contributed to psychotherapy. This work of healing brings together science and religion and it should contribute to a closer co-operation between priest and medical practitioner. I am not bound to any particular school of analysis, but follow wherever the sick person takes me; he leads, I follow. Sometimes I am taken into the land of Freud, at another time it may be that of Jung. My mainstay is dream analysis, and as the person's pattern of life becomes increasingly clarified so does health return. The dream is seen as revealing a pattern both in the general or manifest way and also in a much more subtle manner which calls upon as much intuition as possible from the analyst, as well as a considerable store of psychological knowledge. Free association is used in the interpretation of dreams and of the other material used, such as drawings and paintings. I have concluded a long analysis by means of drawings alone.

I shall best serve my purpose by showing you the kind of person who has been helped to discover a new and full life. There are the students with their problems. An undergraduate came to me whose distracted mind was so acute that he was unable to attend lectures or do any work; in fact he spent most of the day wandering round the city in a dazed condition. Such thoughts as he had were of a religious nature and they settled upon the idea of the Second Coming. He felt that if only he could settle this problem everything else would be happy for him. When he came to see me all he wished to discuss was the Second Coming, and he was completely unaware of the real unconscious problem which was endangering his future. The treatment was lengthy, but in the end he obtained a degree, and today he is happily married and teaches in a grammar school.

Sometimes the cause of a mental breakdown seems to arise within the Church, although in fact the real cause lies far back in infancy. Several young people came to me in quick succession who had been attending a place of worship where the Great Judgement Day and Hell Fire were vigorously preached; this preaching brought to a head guilt which had long been simmering in the unconscious mind. They definitely required treatment, and this they received.

I am particularly interested in those people whose emotional disorder produces physical symptoms. Helping to heal these is particularly satisfying, for not only does it show again the closest connection between mind and body but also everyone can see what has been achieved, whereas fears and worries and headaches have nothing much to show for their removal. One such person was Mrs. X, who at the cost of much time and money had been given frequent examinations at her local hospital; finally she was sent for an examination to a well-known professor at a certain university. He told her she had "double optic atrophy" and that nothing whatever could be done to restore her sight. For years she went about groping her way in a state of semi-blindness. Clutching at any straw, as such people are wont to do, she came to see if I could help her. It was soon evident, in her history, that there was sufficient material to cause such hysterical blindness. Her treatment lasted a considerable time, nevertheless she slowly improved, and today she has, in the words of her optician, "vision as good as could be expected for her age". For two years now she has read her daily newspaper and she is a regular television viewer. There were certain events in her life before which she had drawn a blind, and her loss of outward vision was but an expression of her loss of inward vision.

A wife in her early thirties had numerous examinations at her local hospital and she was given drugs with no effect. She was convinced she was full of cancer. Finally, she was told by the hospital that her trouble was psychological. Under treatment her real cancer was found to be of a moral kind which was expressing itself in pain; also, the pain served as an act of self-imposed atonement. The treatment is continuing; the pains have almost gone, and happier relationships have arisen within her family.

As many men as women come for help. There was a young man who upon qualifying in his profession gave up his career to "go in for music", which in the main consisted of playing in a jazz band. The thought of marriage filled him with panic, he was indecisive, a worrier, he felt people to be critical of him, so he contracted out of society and felt the unreality of everything. His father was an atheist, his mother deeply religious; he, in rebellion against his mother, called himself an agnostic. Today he is married most happily, he is back at his professional work, and through the help the Church has brought him he became confirmed, and he has considered ordination. His wife, who like her husband was outside the Church, joins him in regular worship and in the activities of the Church.

Mr. A. was a man in his forties: from a very poor home he rose to a high position in high-grade technical work. The day came when he was in the running for an appointment to a managership of a factory, but it was then that he contrived unconsciously to have an accident which put him out of the running for the position. He could not face the possibility of a failure, so he unwittingly provided himself with an excuse: "I could have risen to the top, but my accident prevented me." There was much more to his trouble than that, for he felt in every way inadequate, particularly in regard to his family, where he thought of himself as "a worm and no man". This sense of inferiority produced in him the most intense aggression towards his wife and children, and he went in daily fear of murdering them. Such cases are quite frequent, and to know such a person intimately makes one feel something of the sheer terror which makes his life a burden. He is today doing very well indeed, and he has been selected for a task which would tax the ability of any man, and all is happy at home.

Two young men are having treatment, each of whom has a Ph.D. degree. One of them found himself living and working in an unreal world. He could not get to grips with his work, and the same was true of his religious life. There is the usual guilt, but a major factor in his story is the question of vocation. As he faces the main decision of his life's work, his decisiveness is returning.

A young man was behaving badly in the youth organisation of his church, and as time went by his aggression became alarming. His condition was serious, but he came through it all a new man and he expresses his profoundest gratitude for the help received.

Then, of course, there are many people who are weighed down by incessant worries. When they have got rid of one worry they needs must find something else about which to worry. Similarly, we can help those many people who suffer from depression, or from headaches which often have the intensity of migraine, or those who cannot sleep, or who wake up each morning feeling more tired than when they went to bed. And so we might go on to aid the homosexual, the fetishist or the obsessional.

These examples of healing which have come from the Church are by no means exhaustive in the type of sickness which may receive a cure. It seems as though any physical disorder may be produced as a symptom of an underlying emotional sickness, although one would never assume that all the ills which affect the body are caused psychologically. The vast majority of the cases of "mental sickness" may be assumed to have a cause which can be unearthed and healed by the bringing together of science and religion in this way.

I wish to turn now to the challenge and the opportunity which this work presents to the Church of our day. It presents one of the best evangelistic opportunities, for people who are so fundamentally helped by the Church are not likely to forget the benefits received at her hands. A lady who was cured of her asthma not only became a regular member of her church but on account of the transformation of the home life her husband came, and her two sons, one of whom is hoping to be ordained; all of them have been regular members for six or seven years. People ask, "What is the good of the Church?" Here at least they can see the Church in action in a most practical manner when, in their condition, only such mighty works done in the name of the Lord will impress them. I am convinced that over a number of years through this most personal work a congregation can be built up of people who have received such benefits from the Church.

It must be mentioned here that during analysis one has to keep a strict neutrality or else the treatment may break down. It is in the closing stages of the treatment, when the person has almost come through all the wood into the light of a new day, that the evangelistic opportunity begins to present itself.

Further, the help given is not just the removal of unpleasant symptoms—there is a gain of vision, of new understanding of fellow man, and of a deepened spirituality in the people who have undergone a lengthy treatment. They are not only better in the common meaning of the word, but they are fundamentally better people for what they have experienced in the therapy. In analysis people are stripped of every pretence and insincerity; it is a "root and branch" matter, whereas so much of our ordinary pastoral work is superficial.

Then think of the loss of efficiency which the Church suffers through absence on account of sickness in the members. Every Sunday and every week-day in our organisations people are absent through such illness as could be healed by the Church's exercising of such a ministry. There would no longer be cases of people who have strange "turns" whenever they go to church and so "never go these days", nor would there be those people who are "too nervous" to take part in the life of the parish church.

When this work is done manifestly without any motive of gain no one can resist the fact that Christ Himself is being revealed in it. And although there are disadvantages arising from free treatment yet surely these are more than compensated for by the fact that the whole work of healing, involving as it often does many months of very frequent interviews, needs not to be advertised as the work of Christ Himself. It speaks for itself.

We do not suggest that every parish priest or minister should take up this ministry; there is much other work to be done besides, and not every person is fitted for it. The framework of the Church of England, with its compact parochial system, leaves little room for such work as things are at present. Surely the compassion of Christ constrains us to make room for centres within every diocese where this work can be carried on and where advice can be given to the parochial clergy in dealing with sick persons under their care. The need is enormous, and perhaps the chief burden of the work is having to refuse help to people who are desperate and whose burden of suffering makes one's heart bleed. The demands are beyond one's capacity to meet; this is borne out here by the readiness of some people to give up their work and settle in Leicester, taking temporary work, in order to receive this help from the Church. They are waiting at the doors of our churches to find from Christ that healing which came from Him long ago and which He commissioned His Church to perform.

7

CO-OPERATION IN DIVINE HEALING

by THE REV. DR. F. E. ENGLAND

Dr. England, M.A., Ph.D., is an ordained minister of the Presbyterian Church, and is now minister in charge of the Church at Bexhill-on-Sea. For many years he has been a Lecturer and Examiner for the University of London Department of Extra Mural Studies, in psychology and kindred subjects. He is the author of many articles on Psychology and Divine Healing.

I HAVE described my theme as co-operation in *Spiritual* or Divine Healing because I believe that fundamentally all healing is spiritual. There is no form of illness that is not an impairment of the whole person and whether he be in a casualty ward or in the X-ray room, whether a surgical or a medical case, whether a neurotic or an alcoholic, the treatment he needs is a comprehensive treatment resulting in the restoration of his full integrity as a complex spiritual being.

Although there is considerable evidence of a co-operation at informal levels between individual doctors and clergy, it is not easy to see how it could be organised in any systematic way. Doctors and clergy appear to work in different fields; or if they actually occupy one and the same field, their basic principles, though not necessarily incompatible, are certainly different. Ever since the dethronement of the medicine man the physician has tended to rely on the principle of natural causation which underlay the medicine man's use of medicaments, while the priest retained the supernaturalism which was probably the more important and effective factor in primitive treatment.

It must be admitted, I think, that the works of healing recorded in the New Testament come within the priestly category. While the physicians of Greece were assiduously following the lead given in scientific medicine by Hippocrates, Jesus laid his hands on the sick and healed them. And it was by the finger of God that the apostles conceived themselves to be carrying out Christ's command to heal the sick. Some of them, notably Peter and John, were conspicuously successful. We know, also, from the Epistle of St. James, that prayer and anointing were used by the elders of the Church in cases of sickness.

It would not be true, however, to say that the Church's function in relation to sickness has always been conceived exclusively in terms of "spiritual healing" in the sense of prayer and anointing. For centuries the Christian Church played a leading part in the Ministry of Healing by scientific methods. From the days of Constantine the building and equipping of hospitals was energetically carried out by the Church; the monasteries became centres of healing, and in many of their gardens various herbs were cultivated for the preparation of the necessary medicaments.

Gradually, however, the vocation of healing passed into the hands of professional men who derived their inspiration less from Christ than from Hippocrates, and the breach between the care of the body and the care of the soul widened. And although the Church has continued, especially through its excellent medical missions, to sponsor the work of physical healing, and although the medical missionaries carry on their work in close association with the preaching of the Gospel, the treatment of bodily illness has followed the normal scientific methods.

In recent years, however, largely because of increased attention to personal, and particularly emotional, factors in illness, it has become impossible to make a clear-cut distinction between the disorders of the body and those of the soul. Psychological

95

investigation and treatment unearthed a wide range of psycho-somatic disorders, while faith healers have succeeded in reproducing some of the miracles of the New Testament.

One important result is that a growing number of people feel that it is the responsibility of the Church to recover and use the apostolic gift of healing by purely spiritual means. But a cleavage has taken place between those who envisage Spiritual Healing apart from scientific healing and those who see the importance of collaboration between the two. I personally feel that despite the difficulties that lie in the way of co-operation every effort should be made to promote it.

There is no need to stress the danger involved in the mere removal of symptoms, whether psychological or organic, by means of powerful religious suggestion without reference to the underlying causes of these symptoms. Nor is it necessary to do more than utter a *caveat* against the extravagant claims sometimes made by faith healers. One need mention only one of the many factors that may play their part in a "cure". The *vis medicatrix naturae* (nature's own curative power) is such that not infrequently a pathological condition clears up in a manner not understood by the physician. I myself know a man in the eighties upon whom the death sentence was passed several years ago. According to the most expert diagnosis, made independently by two eminent consultants, he was then suffering from an inoperable cancer. Today the same consultants agree that the symptoms have disappeared. The general practitioner makes no claim to have cured the patient by medical treatment, nor does the man himself claim to have been cured by extra-medical means.

One very important consideration is that a great number of illnesses, not necessarily psycho-genic, are more likely to meet their cure if and when the patient is free from hampering moods of fear, surrender and hopelessness, and in this way spiritual ministrations may contribute to a satisfactory recovery. It is not difficult to see the part played by "morale", in the highest sense of the term, in some of the New Testament work of healing. In the Jewish world of the first century the impact of psychic and spiritual influences would be more externally effective than in our day. A generation not yet infected by the cool critical spirit of science possessed more credulity, greater suggestibility and more readiness to respond to spiritual authority than is common today. Often the typical conflict is described in terms of demon-possession. A good example is the man with the unclean spirit described in Mark 1: 23 and Luke 4: 33. Both use the word *akathartos* to denote the man's condition, and the word *exousia* to denote the power of the healer. *Akathartos* denotes an impure (i.e. disharmonious) state. The man's integrity was broken. "Let *us* alone," he cried; "what have *we* to do with thee?" There is also a suggestion of the presence of some faint desire to recover the missing unity. "*I* know thee, who thou art, the Holy One of God." The stricken man, while clinging to his plurality, is still able feebly to assert his integrity. Appealing to that lingering remnant of the man's real self, Christ's attack upon the complex produced a fierce resistance culminating in the smashing of the complex before unity and peace were achieved. Both narrators attribute the cure to a new power, and Luke significantly tells us (4: 32) that the source of the new power was Christ's Gospel.

There we have a distinct pointer to Christ's method and purpose in Spiritual Healing. His miracles cannot be detached from His central vocation as Saviour. They were never mere demonstrations of occult powers. They were, as St. John says, "works of God"; they were signs of God's action; part of Christ's purpose to give men fullness of life by bringing them into touch with God. When He said, "Take up thy bed and walk," He also said, "Thy sins be forgiven thee." His essential ministry was a ministry neither of teaching alone, nor of preaching, nor of healing. It was a ministry of reconciling men to God. He gave of the strength and love of His personality to lame, needy, sick people, healing their diseases, supplying their needs, teaching them, but always with the direct

D

97

object of mediating God to them in and through His devoted self.

In more than one place a vivid contrast is presented between the lesser gift of physical soundness and the greater gift of spiritual wholeness. For example, of the ten lepers it is said that as they went they were *cleansed*, but only the one who came back was made spiritually whole (Luke 17: 19). I venture to think that the New Testament narrators sometimes give the impression that Christ was concerned with physical healing for its own sake. But after allowing for His deep humanitarian interest, it remains that His supreme purpose was to lift all men, sick and well alike, to the full stature of sons of God and to remove every obstacle in the way of its attainment.

Today we have innumerable agencies for the uplift of men, and among them the medical services occupy a distinguished place. In child-guidance clinic, in school and club, as well as in hospital, more than ever is being done to release and ennoble the spirit of man. Where now is the place for Spiritual Healing? It is not suggested that it should be confined to that department of life which remains untouched by the social services. If it be true that the human individual is an indissoluble whole, any defect at any level is an impairment of that whole. And since the apex of the pyramid of a man's being is his spirit, the spiritual healer is concerned with all levels.

It is perhaps inevitable that the function of the spiritual healer should be determined by his conception of the status and functions of the ministry as such. According to one view, the spiritual healer is a priest, holding a commission to administer a supernatural grace. He may be set apart for the work of spiritual healing by virtue of his possession of certain charismatic gifts evidenced by results. He may have the greatest respect for scientific methods of healing, but he will normally act independently of such methods, or at most in a manner supplementary to them. There will be no concrete basis of co-operation between him and the medical men.

On the other hand, those who take a different view of orders

98

will normally conceive themselves to be working in the same sphere as that of the physician but on another level. They will seek to gain an ever-deepening understanding of the spiritual factors in healing at every level. They will rely on the medical man (including the psychiatrist) for a more or less complete case-history and a regular diagnosis, and they will concentrate mainly upon the moral and spiritual factors in illness. It is with this kind of Spiritual Healing that the medical profession might be expected to co-operate.

On a basis of a long experience of active co-operation with general practitioners and psychiatrists, and of close observation of other healing ministries, I unhesitatingly say that Spiritual Healing is most effective and satisfactory not in the realm of organic disease so much as in the matter of personal adjustment. At the former level, indeed, part of the function of Spiritual Healing may well be to help the sufferer to adopt a wise attitude towards his affliction, facing it without fear and adjusting his thought, feeling, and will so as to lay himself open to the process of healing. No small part of the value of spiritual treatment lies in inculcating a right attitude towards suffering. Probably few people in these days are victims of the ancient belief that all suffering is punitive, but many people find a stone of stumbling in the very existence of suffering. They regard pain as an enemy and not as a friend, a signal, a sign of maladjustment. The faith healer as such is usually content to remove the pain; the physician regards pain as a valuable clue to the discovery of the cause; the spiritual healer cannot ignore the positive value that often resides in pain and suffering. St. Paul at first regarded his thorn in the flesh as a source of vexation and he thrice prayed that it might be removed. He was disposed to think of it as "a messenger of Satan to buffet him". But he came to see that, rightly regarded, his inevitable infirmity might be made the means of a richer experience of the sustaining grace of God, and in that wise state of acquiescence he received the blessed assurance, "My grace is sufficient for thee; for my strength is made perfect in weakness" (2 Cor.

99

12: 9). This implied no passive resignation; it meant that the pain, instead of being resented, was turned to spiritual gain. Every hospital chaplain feels happy when he has been able to get a patient to see and believe that there is a frustration that ennobles; giving while it seems to take away, and enriching while it appears to deprive.

But there is an even more thorough-going adjustment, to secure which is the special task of the spiritual healer. Normally the aim of the doctor is the restoration of healthy organic functioning; the aim of the psychiatrist is a well-balanced personality free from inhibition, or dissociation, or conflict. The spiritual healer likewise considers bodily and mental health to be a desirable value, but he declines to give even mental health the premier place, for two main reasons. First, he believes that the value of mental health is considerably reduced if and when it is regarded negatively as mere freedom from conflict. The moment we ask what positive characteristics the healthy person is expected to possess we raise the problem of other values. Plato said of the citizens of his ideal city that one of the essential virtues was health of mind, and that for the rank and file this same health of mind was evinced by a willingness to acquiesce without question in the rule of their guardians. Probably our contemporary dictators hold a similar view of healthy-mindedness in the citizens of the totalitarian states. Such a view rests, however, not upon psychological considerations pure and simple, but upon a definite political theory. And it will be found that any further attempt to define the positive elements in the healthy personality will draw upon values which are, to say the least, other than individual.

In the second place, the spiritual healer believes that all personal and social values depend ultimately upon certain *a priori* values which are grounded in the nature of things. The superiority of the healthy life over the unhealthy, the desirability of ordering life in accordance with the "reality-principle" rather than the "pleasure-principle", our preference for beauty rather than ugliness, and for social unity rather than anarchy—these and all other utilitarian values rest in the last resort upon a philosophy of life, a metaphysics, which takes into account those elements in a man's total environment which link him with that spiritual order in the light of which alone the deepest things of his spirit become intelligible. It is man's adjustment to this wider, this ultimate environment that is the true end of Spiritual Healing, and this supreme step is taken at the instigation of a religious faith that goes far beyond either psychological suggestion or scientific hypothesis.

It is a faith based on insight; it is a personal response to spiritual reality; it is the throwing open of the door of one's whole being to God. It is not a fleeting thing dependent on our moods; it is a conviction rooted in man's apprehension of God. It is grounded on the confidence that in a world where man is continuously urged to move higher, to aspire to greater things, to cherish lofty ideals of personal and social conduct, we are justified in believing that at the heart of it all is a Being who is calling men into fellowship with Himself.

The theology of it will be variously expressed, but the kernel of it is the same for all believers. The specific task of the spiritual healer is to help people to make the contact, and sometimes this needs the most penetrating insight into the reasons for the want of contact. They are, of course, legion; but their common name is sin—sin in the New Testament sense of estrangement from God. In many instances the estrangement is the product of sheer neglect or spiritual insensitiveness. In others it springs from a sense of guilt.

It is in respect of the treatment of a sense of guilt that much research is needed in order to bring the psychiatrist and the spiritual healer into closer co-operation. One may roughly distinguish three kinds of wrongdoing which may be accompanied by a sense of guilt. The first consists in transgression of eternal command or law. The second is a deviation from a man's own judgement of the right or the good. The third is sin, in the New Testament sense of estrangement from God.

The situation is complicated by the fact that all three kinds of wrongdoing are capable of producing spurious as well as genuine guilt feelings. At the authoritarian level a genuine feeling of guilt attaches itself normally to anti-social conduct; but there are attitudes towards authority which produce spurious guilt feelings which may or may not resemble those of the *Oedipus* complex. At the level of moral conduct the sense of guilt or innocence is directly related to the individual's envisagement of moral ends. It follows that if those ends or ideals are primitive, the sense of guilt will be defective and the guilt symptoms will attach themselves to all manner of trivial aberrations.

At the religious level the consciousness of sin and the feeling of personal guilt that goes with it will vary with different degrees of spiritual sensitiveness. To an Isaiah, vividly aware of the awesome presence of the Most Holy God, the sense of personal defilement is acute. At the other end of the scale are guilt feelings of a dubious kind, especially where the actual object of the individual's religious feeling is not the true and living God but a mere system of ideas. At this level guilt-feelings are sometimes childish, sometimes neurotic, sometimes morbid. Everyone who is in close contact with elderly women (mostly unmarried) knows how prevalent is the consciousness of having committed the unpardonable sin—a state of mind that is attended by the profoundest remorse or fear. Often in cases of ideational obsession, profane or obscure ideas will intrude upon a devotional exercise, and the subject, finding himself unable to dislodge the obnoxious intruders, suspects in his nature a deep-seated perversion which denotes an incurable defilement. In many cases the morbid sense of inexpiable guilt arises from the fact that the actual object of the individual's devotion is little more than his own objectified super-ego.

Now the psychiatrist's business in regard to all these types of spurious guilt feelings is to try to help the patient to grow up emotionally by disentangling the primitive attitudes, casting out the lingering remains of archaic authoritarianism, breaking through the vicious circle of frustration, fear, hostility, guilt, and renouncing the neurotic guilt which consists in remorse at having failed to repress and control the morbid concept.

I venture to say that in the best interests of the patient the spiritual healer will not try to by-pass this phase of the treatment, nor seek to nullify the psychological causation by imposing upon it a yet more powerful mechanism of repression. His principal concern will be to lift the whole problem above the level of psychology or of morality. He will rejoice in the removal of neurotic guilt, but he will never accept the finished product of psycho-analysis, or electro-convulsive therapy, or leucotomy, as the end of the healing process. On the contrary, he will view the situation as a swept and garnished house ready for the entry of seven devils or of the Spirit of Life in Jesus Christ. He may even intensify the genuine sense of guilt by bringing it into the awful light of God's holiness, but only to find it melted by the grace of forgiveness and the blessing of absolution. His principal and final aim is to bring the patient into vital relationship with God and with all those spiritual influences which will put him on the high road to the realisation of his true destiny as a child of God and heir of eternity.

The spiritual healer is aware, as St. Peter was, that it is not by his own power or holiness that he restores this "perfect integrity" (Acts 3: 16) to people. His function is to bring people into contact with what St. Paul vividly described as "the divine dynamic which makes for wholeness" (Rom. 1: 16). His task is not merely to supplement medical work but to care for the sick souls of men; not merely to relieve pain, but to raise men's lives to moral and spiritual dignity; to place a new valuation upon men by treating them as children of God, spiritually sick and needing the love of Christ; to saturate all remedial work with His spirit, to do what Swinburne finely said of Catherine of Sienna:

"... In her sacred saving hands
She took the sorrows of the lands.
With her maiden palms she lifted up
The sick times blood-embittered cup.
And in her virgin garment furled
The faint limbs of a wounded world."

8

CO-OPERATION BETWEEN THE MEDICAL PROFESSION AND THE CHURCH

by MISS A. GRAHAM IKIN

Miss Ikin, M.A., M.Sc., was formerly Organising Secretary and Lecturer for the Archbishop of York's Committee of Doctors and Clergy, and also for the National Council for Pastoral and Medical Co-operation. Through these offices she has played an outstanding part in drawing together doctors and clergy that they may understand each other's work in the total Ministry of Healing. She is the author of many books, including Religion and Psychotherapy, The Background of Spiritual Healing, New Concepts of Healing, *and* Victory Over Suffering.

FOR MANY YEARS my work has been concerned with the co-operation of doctors and clergy, and as a result of my experience this essay is set out in three sections. The first shows the importance of psychological and spiritual factors in life and health. The second section considers practical co-operation between Christian doctors and clergy in the present experimental stage. The third section shows something of the part played by prayer in healing sickness and maturing personality.

THE IMPORTANCE OF PSYCHOLOGICAL AND SPIRITUAL FACTORS IN LIFE AND HEALTH

In *Man the Unknown* Dr. Alexis Carrel, a Nobel Prize holder, has said: "There are, as we know, two kinds of health: natural and artificial. Scientific medicine has given to man artificial health and protection against most infectious diseases. It is a marvellous gift. But man is not content with health that is only lack of malady and depends on special diets, chemicals, endocrine products, vitamins and periodical medical examinations, and the expensive attention of hospitals, doctors and nurses. He wants natural health, which comes from resistance to infectious and degenerate diseases, from equilibrium of the nervous system. . . . Artificial health does not suffice for human happiness" (pp. 284–5).

The attempt to separate the physical and spiritual aspects of life has been disastrous. When doctors were primarily concerned with the functions of the body and clergy and ministers with the destiny of our souls, the *unity* of the real human person was lost. The great increase of mental and nervous disorders in the modern world is in part due to this lack of a central inner control that is expressed in the harmony of physical, mental and spiritual health.

Medical psychology, or psychiatry as its practical application is called, has opened the way to a deeper understanding of the part played by mental and spiritual factors in the health of the body and mind. It has also opened the way to a realisation that physical factors, such as acute infections or injury to the brain, can cause mental and spiritual disturbances which no amount of psychological treatment or spiritual exhortation can influence through the mind of the sufferers, but which can be modified by physical means.

A more comprehensive science must be developed to *include* mental and spiritual activities as operative within the organism as a whole, within man as a social and personal being; together with a religious attitude that allows for and includes the effects on mental and spiritual activities of physical conditions, both internally and environmentally.

The revival of the Ministry of Healing within many branches of the Church has coincided with this development into the sphere of the psyche from the medical side. It illustrates the over-spill of the spiritual into the physical rather than its independence of it. It is also bringing the realisation that healthy bodies and minds are more effective instruments for spiritual activities and development than sick ones can ever be. The old idea that God sent sickness to be endured patiently is incompatible with Christ's healing work which showed the compassion of God for sufferers.

Health, whether of body, mind or spirit, is a positive attribute. It is a harmonious balance or interplay between the individual organism or person and the environment within which it functions. Disease involves a breakdown of this, whether through the invasion of specific disease germs, or mental and emotional conflicts within the individual that sap the vitality needed for creative living.

Psychosomatic medicine has developed from the medical side as doctors began to realise the vast problem set by diseases caused by emotional stresses, anxieties and worries. Doctors, however, cannot always remove the causes of distress within the emotional and mental life of their patients. The ministry of the Churches can help here.

No one approach is adequate to the richness and variety of our heritage. God works *precisely*: not vaguely. Pious uplift is no substitute for knowledge based on experience, skill and insight. Doctors are trained to use drugs that are dangerous in excess. They must know not only *what* to administer, but *how much*. The surgeon's skill depends upon his knowledge of the anatomy and physiology of the body, as well as upon his control of his emotions and his hands. The psychotherapist must know in *detail*, not in generalities, the personal history and experience of his patients in order to cure disorders that have led to a breakdown. Often some superficially insignificant fact may uncover a deep-rooted resistance. When this can be "seen through" a patient's attitude may be radically and permanently changed for the better. So, too, a spiritual director needs to know the specific sins and temptations that hinder the full development of spiritual life if he is to help anyone to discover and live from his own true spiritual centre. Psychiatry and spiritual direction over-lap. Each has a contribution to make to our growing knowledge of the nature of man.

In *Victory over Suffering*[1] I wrote: "Man is more than his body or his emotions. There is at the centre of our real being a point of contact with a world of spirit which transcends the space and time within which our minds and bodies function. Man is only truly and fully himself when this is in harmony with the mental and physical laws which give rise to healthy mental and physical functioning. Surgeons can operate, doctors can replace certain deficiencies by means of drugs, vitamins and hormones. Psychiatrists can probe the mind. But true healing comes from God through this hidden spiritual centre of our being. Doctors may call it nature: but God is more than nature left to itself. There is a science of physical functioning—physiology. There is a science of mental functioning—psychology. But there is no adequate or agreed science of spiritual processes, which are even more fundamental for man's welfare. Yet it is within this sphere, I am convinced, ultimate healing for body, mind and spirit must come. We are only on the fringe of realising the possibilities that lie ahead."

This, however, brings us to the next section.

DOCTORS AND CLERGY

In spite of greatly increased awareness of the over-lapping of the spheres within which doctors, psychologists and clergy work, the time is not yet ripe for co-operation on the grand scale, with the medical profession and the churches in harmony. On the one hand doctors have to treat patients of all denominations and of none: people with religious faith and those without it. But even if the medical profession could accept spiritual therapy, or healing through prayer as at least as relevant as psychotherapy, the churches themselves are too divided and unsure of their competence in this field to be relied upon as

[1] *Victory Over Suffering*, published by Arthur James (Evesham).

a whole by doctors: though many recognise the work that is being done by some ministers and clergy in this field.

The medical profession has specialised in treating the sick. Large-scale hospitals make provision for many kinds of help: including hospital chaplains. Yet with all this many are chronically ill, many are mentally ill, and many more are spiritually bankrupt.

This is, or should be, the direct concern of the churches. "What is the Church doing to let people get into this condition?" A young doctor in a mental hospital once said to me, "They come to us too late." The question is still a challenge.

If full-scale co-operation is not yet practicable because the churches are not yet in a position to offer it, in spite of their potential resources and present attempts to draw upon these, what can be done to prepare the way for it?

Three practical levels of co-operation between doctors and clergy developed under the aegis of the Archbishop of York's Committee of doctors and clergy, and the National Council for Pastoral and Medical Co-operation, which included the late Dr. Temple and Lord Horder.

1. Groups of doctors and clergy met to see what kind of co-operation was possible in their daily work. As they came to know each other and discovered each other's capacities, they found many more opportunities of calling on the services of one another for individual cases.

2. The second level of co-operation is illustrated by the medical staff of a mental hospital joining with clergy in regular conferences at which I lectured and then opened a discussion. In return the medical staff invited the clergy to the hospital. The principle of giving clergy some clinical experience in hospitals is much further developed in America than over here.

Moreover, as a result of another group of doctors and clergy one Free Church minister was attached to the psychiatric department of the university, to practise psychotherapy as a pastor, not a doctor. That is a precedent that should be extended.

3. The third level of actual co-operation was an exploration of the field from the specialist level. Research groups of consultants, psychiatrists and clergy met to consider a number of problems met with in the course of their work which could not be dealt with adequately without expert knowledge on a level not primarily within their competence.

One of the greatest difficulties here was to focus the real issues in a way that was intelligible to both professions. It seemed as if each was tunnelling through the same mountain starting from opposite sides and from different levels. Effective co-operation involves mutual understanding and awareness of the contributions possible from both sides.

In the meantime, while the pundits may differ and explore, what can be done by doctors, clergy and congregations as they are to help actual sufferers in their need?

First it is essential to realise the "diversity of gifts" and training through which the Spirit works.

The first step towards effective co-operation between doctors and clergy is a recognition of, and respect for, their different contributions to the well-being of patient or parishioner.

Once when seriously ill myself, I asked for communion. My doctor was afraid it would be too much for me, as I was too weak even to feed myself. However, I insisted. When the doctor came the day afterwards he found me very much better and said, "Well, if communion has that effect on you, you can have it every day!" My reply was that if I'd sought it for that, it would not have had such an effect.

The inner attitude and condition of the patient is primary. Doctor or priest are secondary, and it is for them to facilitate the integrity necessary to respond to and draw upon such resources as are available both physically and spiritually.

A further level of co-operation between doctors and clergy involves this field in which a spiritual ministry may have startling results physically. There is no need here to quote examples. They are widespread, and more clergy and ministers are realising a responsibility for developing and extending a healing ministry. More doctors also are finding that results which go beyond what they would have expected from their own approach do at times occur. Many doctors are sceptical, suspecting faulty diagnoses, or that the symptoms were hysterical or the cure due to suggestion. They have every right to be cautious in the interests of their patients. Clergy, ministers or lay healers with a charismatic gift need to be careful in their claims if they are to win credence for the reality of a further reinforcement through the Spirit that can profoundly modify psychosomatic conditions, in organic as well as functional conditions. Dr. Alexis Carrel, however, won the Nordhoff-Jung medal for cancer research, so he is not likely to be mistaken in his diagnosis of cancer. Yet he claims to have seen cancerous sores disappear very rapidly under his eyes after earnest prayer. He said it seemed to involve an enormous speeding up of cicatrization. He is convinced from his own experience that healing through prayer is a reality, and that prayer is "the most powerful form of energy that one can generate". This leads us to the next section.

THE REALITY OF PRAYER

Much has been written on prayer, much more remains to be explored. The God who makes the stars with their flaming energies on so large a scale and yet brings a human child with all its potentialities for mature manhood into existence through a single cell cannot be adequately known in a day, or even a lifetime. The more one learns of Him, the more we realise there is to discover. St. Paul well referred to the "unsearchable riches of Christ".

We have referred to the work of doctors, nurses and all the equipment and personnel in hospitals for the treating of the sick. We know that if an accident happens an ambulance will soon be on the spot and all that can be done physically for the injured person will be done. This secular organisation is effectively operated throughout the country.

How can the Churches add to this? Many ventures and experiments are being made today by people who have found that through prayer greater resources become available than on the purely natural level. Healing work for minds as well as bodies goes on through small groups of people who join together to pray for those who are ill or in distress. If every parish and every Free Church congregation had such a praying fellowship on which *all* its members could count if their need arose, as they can count on doctor and ambulance, the results would be very far-reaching. "Where two or three are gathered together in MY NAME," said CHRIST, "there am I in the midst of them." We must bring the *specific* needs of individual people within the range of intercessory prayer. Vague prayers such as "God bless Auntie", which are legitimate in infancy, have to be replaced by a real taking of "Auntie's" needs sufficiently deeply into our *own* hearts to stir a compassion that impels us to reach out in prayer to *our* Father, to meet the need. The human link is necessary as a channel for a divine compassion greater than our own to reach through to meet the particular need.

Effective intercession is no magic turning of a prayer wheel. It is a real link between those for whom we pray, ourselves and God. The intercessor is like the switch that connects the particular light bulb, cooker, or what have you, to the grid with power to work it. The current has to go through the switch! Effective intercession depends on our imagination and compassion being sufficiently stirred to mobilise our attention and resources to be amplified and used by God. It is no magic formula of words, but a vital link between our awareness of human need and of divine resources greater than our own on which to draw to meet it.

God works through a fellowship. The fellowship of the Holy Spirit is a fellowship that transcends denominational difference, race, age or sex, amongst those who have found in Christ the break-through into time of the Eternal Spirit in whom our own lives are rooted. All *human* differences, real and important as these are in their own place, are negligible in our relation to God. We are *all* in the same boat there; our dependence on the divine ground of our being is absolute. All other relations are relative.

Medical, psychological and all scientific work falls within this relative sphere, along a horizontal line, so to speak, from past, through the present to the future. Prayer opens up another dimension, which is often symbolised as vertical in relation to the horizontal temporal continuity. It is impossible to prove the reality of this to those completely enclosed within the externalised world of time and space. It is equally impossible to disprove its reality to those who have found a window into Eternity that reflects real illumination and power into the temporal world and transforms it by so doing. The lesser cannot understand or comprehend the greater. The greater can include as well as transcend the lesser.

Those who have become aware of this all-encompassing spiritual Reality, within which our everyday experience is set, become a focus through which God can influence the course of temporal events more directly than through the routine "natural laws" which enable us to count on the regularity of the seasons and the motion of stars and suns.

This is the sphere in which "miracles" of healing can and do occur. This is not by the suspension of natural laws but by bringing into operation higher laws through the love, faith and insight of those who have awakened to another dimension of being which underpins and interpenetrates our human world.

This is the sphere in which the Churches have a positive contribution to bring to the problems of disease and disorder. Although in each age forms of organisation have to vary to meet the social, cultural and practical level of life, there are resources which come from this other dimension of Spirit. These are only available through those who have felt its reality in their own lives. This life can no more be passed on in a text book to be learnt by heart than a baby can be produced by reading a book on parenthood. Life comes from life, spiritually as well as physically. It grows in the living and loving relationships between the more mature and the less mature, until the latter in turn grow up enough to pass it on to others.

To rise to the great challenge set by the threat to civilisation, culture and even life itself on the earth, by hydrogen and atomic bombs, a great fellowship open to the inspiration of the Spirit that makes for harmony, peace and co-operation is needed. We do not want to be told *what* to pray, or even what to pray for. We need to learn *how* to pray so as to become a focus through which God has direct access to the particular situations within which we are set. In so far as we do discover the reality of prayer that opens another dimension of life and experience, in so far as we discover the Kingdom of God that is within us, *we find a real network of praying folk interpenetrating the visible world all the time.* We are inter-connected spiritually as well as organically. Scientific medicine traces out the organic inter-relatedness. Spiritual therapy operates through this invisible yet dynamic network which connects us as persons with our common source in God. *The two approaches are complementary, and for wholeness, both are needed.* If we are tuned in to this spiritual fellowship, awareness of a peace and vitality beyond our everyday levels is as definite as the effects of turning on the electric light with a switch. We know ourselves to be participating in a greater life than our own, in fellowship with many others.

The "communion of saints" in the sense of participation in a life that is shared by those who have passed through the change we call death as well as by those still living on earth, enhances personal life. When this and the "healing of the sick" through the vital energies released spiritually in such a fellowship have become realities in the practice and not just the past history of the Churches, a new age of hope for mankind will be within reach.

An inner nucleus in every church and congregation who are learning to deepen their communion with God through meditation and the contemplation to which it leads, and simultaneously learning how to focus spiritual resources through intercession for others, is essential for the leavening of the Church itself. Within such fellowships it will become as natural to expect the healing of diseases that are as yet incurable on the medical level as it is now to expect and gain relief through medicine and surgery for such ills as they can treat effectively.

This is no "pipe-dream". During the last fifty years many such groups have been demonstrating the power of the Spirit to heal "all manner of diseases". Doctors are co-operating in many places with clergy and ministers who are the spearhead of a praying congregation. The laity are as essential in this healing work as either ordained minister or charismatic healer. We all have a responsibility and cannot just leave it to others. The Spirit is stirring on many levels. Healing work spreads from one to another like a chain-reaction. Will it spread quickly enough to counteract the destructive chain reactions of atomic and hydrogen bombs and prevent them from being used? Spiritual resources are essential for all creative or redemptive work. Spiritual maturity expresses a measure of real harmony between the mind of man and His creator and Redeemer. This is the work of the Holy Spirit who completes the work of Christ in the interior depths of the spirit in us, inspiring us to work and pray for the full coming of the Kingdom of God—of all that is good, lovely and true—on earth as in heaven.

9

THE TRANQUIL MIND

by Dr. Alfred Torrie

*D*r. Torrie, M.A., M.B., Ch.B., D.P.M., is a specialist in *psychiatric medicine, and is a consultant psychotherapist at Napsbury Hospital. He was formerly Superintendent of the Retreat, York, and has been a consultant psychiatrist to H.M. Forces. He is a Fellow of the British Psychological Society, and the author of* The Delinquent Child.

A Mentally Sick Society

DISABILITIES OF THE MIND form nearly half of the diseases treated in the hospitals in Britain, and according to a report from the British Medical Association they are found in one-third of the patients seen by general practitioners in the community. In addition, there are thousands who seek from chemists tranquillising drugs of all kinds for "nerves". Yet there is no evidence that sickness of the mind is increasing today. In 1733 Dr. George Cheyne published a book in which he said that sicknesses of mind "were computed to make almost one-third of the complaints of the people of condition in England".

Recent research has proved that as many days' work are lost in industry through mental sickness as through infections with the common cold. Added to this there are those illnesses, called psychosomatic, caused by strains and stresses and manifested by bodily diseases, especially of the heart and blood vessels. Asthma and migraine have a strong emotional component in their origin. The nervous dyspeptic businessman is frequently found.

THE EFFECT OF SPIRITUAL SICKNESS ON THE BODY AND THE MIND

The distressed mind is not an isolated state. Bodily illnesses affect the mind and vice versa. Sickness of soul can cause distress in the mind and also disability of the body, as the following case history shows:

A man of 45 heard a broadcast church service, but he was listening to it with half his attention. A few days later he complained of indigestion and poor appetite and was out of sorts. A doctor was summoned to his comfortable home. The symptoms of dyspepsia, sleeplessness, etc., were described. An examination revealed no abnormality. The latest indigestion powder was prescribed with no effect. The patient began to fear cancer of the stomach. Depression, anxiety and insomnia began. Admission to a private room in a well-known London teaching hospital followed. Many expensive investigations, such as X-rays, elaborate blood tests, etc., revealed nothing unusual. By now the man was in despair, was sure he was in the grip of an obscure disease which no one could diagnose or cure. He was told that it was his imagination, was sent on a sea voyage, carried his distressed mind and dyspeptic body with him and returned home thinner, more anxious, frightened and with a mind full of morbid and gloomy thoughts. That he was going insane was his main preoccupation. His doctors prescribed tranquillising drugs which made him less anxious but sure now that he was a neurotic wreck.

Finally it was suggested that he should see a psychiatrist. This disturbed him even more and made him terrified of being sent to a mental hospital, and he refused. His wife, a loyal devoted woman with a deep spiritual faith, belonged to a weekly prayer group for Spiritual Healing. The group prayed for the patient and in retrospect one can see that the prayers most certainly made a very great difference to the peace of mind of the patient's wife, whose faith in the ultimate recovery of her husband never wavered.

There was very little progress, however, and two years after the illness I was sent for. Psychiatrists are accustomed to being called in when every other method has been tried. It looked as though a long-established and almost chronic case which could have responded to early treatment might have once more added to the failures of psychiatry. The first problem was that of diagnosis. Many exponents of Spiritual Healing apply a generalised or blunderbus spiritual approach to sickness of mind when a specific problem is present. They do not feel that diagnosis matters. In this case reassurance was given to the patient that as a physician I was interested in the whole man, as a doctor in his body, as a psychiatrist in his mind, and as a fellow child of God in his spirit. This was necessary to allay his fear and distrust of psychiatry.

An examination of his emaciated but still normal body helped to dispel some of his fears. A careful investigation of his medical history, personality, upbringing, background and heredity revealed no evidence of previous sickness of mind in himself or in his family or ancestry. A study of his spiritual development brought the story of a distorted picture of a Calvinistic God who demanded appeasement for sin and whose affronted majesty had to have reluctant forgiveness coerced from Him by good works. His untender and authoritarian father praised him only for scholastic achievements, athletic prowess and assiduous application to the needs of the family business, which he joined on leaving school.

The patient married a gentle, affectionate girl with a personality like that of his mother. He was ambitious for financial success, and sought every opportunity of making social contacts which might increase his business opportunities. His wife saw his increasing preoccupation with climbing up the social ladder with some misgiving. An interview with her revealed various facets of her husband's personality. During their engagement and honeymoon they had read much poetry together. She found he had ideals of serving humanity. These he soon forgot in the fierce competition of the world of business. Frequently he quoted "The race is to the swift and the weakest to the wall". Her gentle expostulations were of no avail. Boasting that he had trebled the family business after his father's death, he was disappointed that she showed little enthusiasm for their increased living amenities.

This was the position when his illness began. The early interviews in treatment consisted in allowing him to tell his story in his own way with few interruptions. The main problem remained: Why did this man's distress of mind begin at the time it did? He confessed himself puzzled and could recall no special noteworthy event about that time. As he proceeded from his physical and mental make-up to his spiritual background we stumbled on to the origin of his unhappiness. He recalled more about the broadcast service which began his troubles. He was reading the City column in a Sunday newspaper. His wife regularly tuned in on Sunday evenings to the church broadcast, although both had long since ceased to belong to any religious body.

After referring to this radio programme he could not for some days remember why it had disturbed him so much. When we came back to the subject he usually exhibited some emotional reaction. Eventually he was given Jung's Word Association test and from the answers it was obvious that he was preoccupied with the idea of death. The morning after our conversation his wife rang to say he had had a very restless night and kept saying over and over again in his sleep, "Thy soul shall be required of thee". Here was a clue and a search of the files of the *Radio Times* brought us to a Sunday service in which one of the readings was in Luke Ch. 12 about the rich man and the building of bigger barns. The discovery led to a rush of recollection.

On that Sunday his wife was regretting the fact that he seemed a changed man and had lost his idealism that appealed so much to her when they were engaged. His reply was to tell her of the many material advantages his success had brought to her. At that time he was planning another expansion of the business. Annoyed that she did not seem enthusiastic about this, he began to sulk. Her words made him feel uneasy and he began justifying himself in his own mind with little satisfaction. His wife then switched on the wireless set and it was during the service to which she was listening that he almost unconsciously caught hold of the phrase "Thy soul shall be required of thee". Formerly an athletic man, his overbusy sedentary office had led to an increase of weight with the usual normal shortness of breath on hurrying upstairs. He wondered if he was going to have heart disease like his father, who was a similar type of man.

All our subsequent meetings were concerned with religious topics. His spiritual hunger was apparent, but its satisfaction was hindered by his ideas of God. These were like the belief of the Spectre's God in William Blake's book "Jerusalem".

> "For he is Righteous, he is not a Being of Pity and
>   Compassion,
> He cannot feel Distress, he feeds on Sacrifice and
>   Offering,
> Delighting in cries and tears . . ."

God in Christ reconciling us frail and fallible men to Himself became for him a longed for but distant God. His commercial mind could not grasp that God's love was given unconditionally, for need and not on merit. Beginning his second forty years of life, his need for adjustment was spiritual, not material or biological. Now that marriage, mating, building the home, parenthood, and providing for his family successfully had passed, he was beginning to turn his thoughts inwards and he had few inner resources to meet his spiritual needs. He now longed for fellowship of a deeper kind with others but for years he had looked upon them as competitors or business rivals. Restoring relationships long since broken by his false sense of values he found difficult. He felt he was isolated and could not buy his way back. He did not possess the necessary currency.

This case has been given at some length to illustrate the interaction between body, mind and spirit. I wish I could record this patient as a psychiatric success but I cannot. His unquietness of mind continued. My constant practice is to pray silently before and often during interviews for healing power to be released in the patient, but my professional pride must have been a stumbling-block. Healing did come, however, for one day he arrived radiantly happy. Now he knew the answer. He had been to a businessmen's Christian union where two colleagues had witnessed to the power of Christ in their lives. The witness included a description of the same weaknesses and selfishness that had afflicted him. I think I failed because perhaps my weakness and selfishness lie in different directions.

THE BODY, MIND, SPIRIT UNITY

The soma, psyche, pneuma integration is for me an essential concept in spiritual healing. Healing, like worship, is threefold. We are asked to love and worship God with heart and mind and soul. Our bodies are the temple of the spirit and the mind is the channel of the soul. Physicians and the clergy are both needed in the campaign to secure tranquillity of mind for our sick society. Materialists insist that we are only bodies, that distress of mind is due to some physical or chemical disturbances of our bodily mechanism, and that our minds are just products of certain electrical changes in the nervous system. These habit patterns follow the conditioning from birth of our inherited tissues. Physical treatment to secure the tranquil mind is their main method of treatment. Psychological theories emphasise the effects of prolonged emotion on the bodily organs. Emotional disabilities from prolonged fear or resentment can affect an organ such as the thyroid gland so severely that a physical treatment of an operative nature may be necessary to deal with the ultimate irreversible effects. Another disease of the thyroid gland causes lack of its secretion and can initiate psychological and spiritual symptoms. The sub-thyroid patient is depressed. All his activities are retarded. His former spiritual awareness is diminished. The giving of thyroid extract removes his depression. He becomes his former cheerful self and his appreciation of spiritual reality returns.

In the case quoted earlier the man who was healthy in body

and mind but spiritually inhibited found wholeness following the release of a nascent response to God. He now sought first the kingdom of the spirit, of right relationships with God and with man, and his health of body and mind returned. Christ became the substance of his hope. The peace of God, its tranquillity and assurance, now became his best medicine. Hope and faith are emotions that, like other emotions, act on the mid-brain, the deep centre which controls the autonomic nervous system, bringing harmony, balance and rhythm to the working of the body and mind.

There is no need to postulate a dichotomy between spirit and the body-mind unit. In the beginning was the primeval cell which through the ages was to become man. In the beginning this primeval cell lived and moved and had its being in God. Ultimately evolution developed a complex system of cells, all having their being in God and in their totality forming the body of man. His nervous system is a more intricate electronic radar than he will ever invent. This receives stimuli or messages from the body, from the mind and *from the spirit*. All our cells are "hid with Christ in God" who is the source of all healing.

THE SEARCH FOR TRANQUILLITY

Men without God are restless until they find rest in Him. They seek goals and satisfactions that still leave them restless. There are four main needs that men try to satisfy hoping to find tranquillity of mind. The *first* is the need for material things which they have in common with the animals—for food, drink, shelter and sexual satisfaction. The multiplicity of ways in which this search is carried out can be seen in many present-day films. The *second* main need which others make their goal is security at any price. The longing for continuity in itself and the fear of change can lead to the death of the spirit and the fate that befell Lot's wife. The hope that tranquillity of mind is achieved by financial success or happiness in marriage alone is belied by our patient's story. The *third* need leads to a more subtle search for peace of mind. It can be seen in what J. B. Priestley calls Admass. This leads to all sorts of pseudo-fellowships giving a feverish and temporary semblance of happiness but leaving out the one thing needful. Real fellowship among men is the result of fellowship with God. Only thus is the threefold relationship achieved. The *fourth* great search for the tranquil mind is found in the urge to create, to invent or to build an empire, a business or other structure. When creation is achieved and the building completed the restlessness returns. "Except the Lord build the house they labour in vain who build it" (Ps. 127: 1).

The satisfaction of one or more of these main needs for material fulfilment, for security, for belonging to the herd and for creative activity can be achieved without bringing the desired goal of the tranquil mind.

Thus far we have seen that tranquillity of mind is bound up with health of body and of spirit. Bodily wellbeing and mental health of themselves may fail to ward off spiritual sickness. Conversely, when health of body and mind are achieved, the doors of the spirit may be opened by the rectifying of a faulty receiving mechanism and a higher level of awareness of spirit results. The body-mind unity is so constructed that action depends on what physiologists call the final common pathway in response to stimuli or impulses coming from the body and the mind and, we would add, the spirit. It is true that a sense of well-being and temporary peace can come purely physically, for instance, after a good meal or the administration of a tranquillising drug. Similar sensations of tranquillity can occur in response to beauty and harmony of sight or sound. Peace of mind can also come from the feeling of safety with familiar things and people, when we are "members one of another". This is a very precious thing but can still leave a vague dissatisfaction and may be but fleeting in its nature. The emotions and bodily sensations alone may be involved. The spirit can still be unhealed.

THE FALSE GOAL OF HEALTH

If bodily health and the tranquil mind are sought as ends in themselves we may still fail to achieve them. The distressed patient already described, and many spiritual healing groups, all seek health as their main goal. The patient had sought not to love God and his neighbour, but to serve himself and his business, and so he fell ill in the way he did. Had he linked himself up with eternal values, which are also the "here and now", he would have been proof against his fear of death. In praying for recovery as the main goal we may be attempting unsuccessfully to by-pass the necessary conditions. "Wilt thou be made whole?"—in body, mind and spirit, and the first and greatest of these is spirit. To become whole in spirit is to be at one with God and to accept His freely offered love. Our patient, a "strictly business" man, could never understand the idea of a gift rather than an exchange transaction. The gift of God's love is costly in a different sense both to the Giver and the receiver. The first step is the receiving, but the next must be one of doing His will whatever befalls. As I see it, our immediate goal in the Spiritual Healing movement is the healing of the spirit, not first the healing of the body and the mind. "Our Father knoweth that we have need of this." Without the surgery of the spirit the rest may not follow. This surgery consists in excising self or, to use an unpopular word, sin.

I saw a girl recently who said she had committed the unforgivable sin—a phrase that is responsible for playing a part in many a suicide. Her interpretation of the phrase and mine were poles apart. Our sins are only unforgivable if we refuse forgiveness. How can God enter if we keep the door shut? Holman Hunt's picture called "The Light of the World" has no handle on the outside of the door so that Christ can only stand and knock. The patient with the idea of having committed the unforgivable sin cannot open the door because she is frustrated by an unconscious wish to punish herself. We can become like

Paul, who boasted that he was the prince of sinners. We claim to judge ourselves and to be our own jury and executioner. We have the arrogance to usurp God who alone can judge and whose vengeance is mercy and love. There are no degrees of sin, large or small. If we place ourselves outside the Kingdom of God, or the Kingdom of right relationships, as somebody called it, it matters little whether we are one inch or one mile outside.

NOT THE WORLD'S PEACE

The peace of mind which the world cannot give brings with it a full harmonious working of the body, mind and spirit unity. This working may be called upon to bear a heavy load, often the burden of frustration of the four needs already referred to. Deprivation of material things, of security in an insecure world, of the relief of loneliness, of outlets for creative gifts, may be a burden which only those who seek to do the will of God can bear with a tranquil mind, as many a missionary could testify. These burdens may work together for good to them that love God. Disease is not the will of God, but when it happens through the sin, folly and ignorance of man, He can, by the gift of Himself, give the tranquil mind in the frustrated body. The mind also may have its strains and stresses but can retain its tranquillity because it is "stayed on God".

SPIRITUAL HEALTH

Finally, the point must be made that prevention of the unquiet mind is better than cure. A body and mind that are at all times open to the Spirit can be raised to the highest state of health so that the resistance to disease is at its maximum. Thus we can link preventive medicine with spiritual health.

Some Spiritual Healing movements remind one of having to call in the fire brigade through not attending to fire precautions. These movements are spreading rapidly, perhaps because, as Christ said, we are "a perverse generation seeking for a sign" but there may be no sign given (Matt. 12:39). These movements have a value in that they are a challenge to the Churches to declare that God works in and through His children everywhere in the bringing in of His Kingdom. They call us back to the belief that there is only one world—God's world—that all life and work is sacramental all the time. When Spiritual Healing movements have done their work there will be no need for them any more, for all Christians will bring health and healing into their daily faith and practice. Thus they will achieve the tranquil mind in a world of turmoil and stress. They will not be spared pain, but this will be lightly borne as they will be sharing a yoke with the Master. As John Wilhelm Rowntree, the Quaker mystic, puts it in a fervent prayer:

> Thou, O Christ, convince us by thy Spirit, thrill us with Thy Divine passion, drown our selfishness in Thy invading love, lay on us the burden of the world's suffering, drive us forth with the apostolic fervour of the early Church.

10

BE HEALED AND MADE WHOLE

by The Rev. Wilfrid H. Bourne

*T*he Rev. W. H. Bourne, F.R.S.A., F.Ph.S., is an ordained
minister of the Methodist Church, who has served in many
parts of the country, and is at present in charge of the Methodist
Church at Selsey. He is a Fellow of the British Federation of
Psychologists, and a Fellow of the Newtonian Society, and the
Founder of "The Guild of Truth". He is the author of many
pamphlets, and a book about his pastoral ministry entitled God
Gave Me a Telephone.

MANY PEOPLE mistakenly think that Christian Healing
cannot be received effectively unless some excep-
tionally gifted "healer" is the ministrant, or unless the
patient is either presented or mentioned in a gathering that is
held for the specific purpose of mediating God's healing power.
Actually there is nothing to prevent the sincere patient from
obtaining this healing grace at home, or in the hospital ward,
or in any other place, when the necessary spiritual conditions
are fulfilled.

The truth of this has been brought home to me on many
occasions. One day a colleague told me of an experience he had
in a Liverpool hospital where during the last war he served as a
male nurse. Passing through one of the women's wards, he saw
a patient reading the Bible and he paused by her bed to speak to
her. She asked him if he believed that God's healing power was
available through prayer and faith; he gave an affirmative reply.
It seemed that the lady had never previously given much

thought to the subject, and had never attended any healing meetings or intercession groups. Now, however, she was thinking much about it but could get no satisfactory answers from her own priest. My friend and the patient talked about Christian Healing for a little while, and he then resumed his journey through the ward.

Later in the day he discovered that his questioner had been diagnosed as suffering from a malignant cancer, and there appeared to be no doubt of the fact. A week later he again visited this lady's ward and spoke to her. She told him that about three days after their previous conversation, as she was praying for healing, a strange feeling of recovery had come to her. My friend again made enquiries and discovered that the surgeons were mystified, for every factor contributing to the original diagnosis had disappeared, and the patient had obtained healing without treatment of any kind. She was discharged from the hospital, and three years afterwards, when she was visited by my colleague, she was, to use his words, "the picture of health".

Another man known to me, a Methodist local preacher, who had been suffering for some time from acute pain in his eyes, underwent a careful examination and was informed that an operation was necessary. A date for this was arranged, and he went home. He and his wife sat late into the night discussing the matter, then, by a flash of inspiration, he had the conviction that no operation was necessary for him. A remedy, he said, had already been provided for those who could believe, and he, as a Christian preacher, should not be unbelieving. Before retiring to bed he and his wife knelt and together they prayed simply that the touch of Jesus might prove its ancient power again. He was awakened during the night by what he termed "a grinding pain" behind his eyes, followed by a feeling that something was breaking up. In a little while these feelings passed and he experienced a wonderful sense of liberation, remarking to his wife that he was convinced that the glaucoma had been completely healed. That conviction was corroborated several days later when he presented himself for an examination preliminary to the expected operation, for every trace of the disease had vanished.

A third instance comes to my mind where no gifted healer or special occasion was involved. An army officer told me that he had succumbed to a mysterious and painful skin disease in the East. In spite of two or three years' treatment by the highest medical authorities the disease had persisted and he had reconciled himself to a lifetime of suffering. Then, in the course of his post-war work as a Christian colporteur, he found himself the guest of a simple village mission worker. The ex-officer told of his painful skin disease and the costly search for effective treatment that had proved unavailing. The villager asked him if, as a Christian, he had ever sought his healing by prayer and faith. The colporteur said he had certainly prayed much for his recovery, but had come to believe it was not God's will that this should result. As they talked together in the little cottage, it came home to him that he had not been sufficiently sensitive to the healing touch of Christ. His notions of God's will had been too rigid, and his views of prayer insufficiently affirmative. His faith had not been directed to God so much as to his disease. He learned a new way of praying in that village home, by which, instead of pleading for the removal of his pain and the disfiguration he loathed so much, he committed himself fully to the healing grace of the Father. He began to affirm his spiritual unity with the Source of all healing and health. Within two weeks no trace of his former disease remained, and it never recurred.

It is, of course, necessary that we have certain convictions. We must believe that God alone is always the Healer, whoever may be serving His gracious work, whether this is doctor, minister, relation, or friend. In the next place we must believe that the will of God is for life, and health, and peace. There should never be the least doubt that the Father's desire is for the broken to be repaired, the lost to be replaced, and the incomplete to be made whole. Then we must know that physical sickness is a visible or felt expression of an inward, invisible cause that is rooted within us; some anxiety, or fear, or sin, or habit that has chafed us spiritually or psychologically until the body itself has become saturated with its action.

Before the outer symptoms and their distresses can be removed, the inner causes have to be dealt with by faith and prayer. We do this in a simple way. Though we may not know what secret underlying cause within us has produced the bodily illness, we can pray for enlightenment leading to its full and final removal. Then, and not till then, the more obvious physical illness, or psychological disturbance, will yield to a happy experience of healing.

We must remember that prayer for bodily healing, as for mental healing, or the forgiveness of sins, can only fitly follow an inward cleansing. Our prior need is for deep changes of thought and life before healing prayers can be effective. Before the body can obtain a healing that can be maintained, the mind and the spirit must be made well. Healing in its *fullness* is our true need: we need to be made *whole*.

In the group intercessions I have led for many years we always pray, in the first place, for this inward cleansing as a preliminary to healing. Our opening prayer is this: "Almighty God, whose will is that life, and health, and peace shall be shared by Thy children on earth, grant unto ourselves, and those for whom we pray, that inner cleansing which must precede Thy healing work. Grant us the freedom we need. Remove the bondage of sin, fear, and anxiety. Search us inwardly as we now confess these hindrances to Thy healing grace, and strengthen the power of Thy Holy Spirit in us. Remove all such infirmities as may hinder the service of healing. Beyond the healing of our bodily and other afflictions bless us with a desire for the renewed mind and the changed heart."

We cannot be healed in body until, first of all, we are inwardly healed. This is one of the reasons for strangely delayed answers to prayers for healing. It is a reason for stubborn resistances in public healing missions. For this reason, also, many relapses occur after healing has seemed to be real. It has been said that the thought of man has so built up the belief in the power and reality of sickness and disease that they seem impregnable fortresses of evil! Those whose faith is in the hold of sickness certainly receive the consequences of that sort of inverted faith, and they cannot avoid them, because it must always be done unto us according to our faith.

There is another conviction that needs to be held, and it is this, that a complete surrender of ourselves, or the dear ones for whom we intercede, must always be made to God. This means that we acknowledge the perfect wisdom as well as the perfect love of God, and His power. Again and again it has been discovered that no progress is made towards healing until this humble surrender has been made. The outcome of our submission to God must be accepted, whatever it should prove to be, and it is necessary that we realise this at the time we pray. *Whatever may follow our prayers, should be received as from the hands of God.* This does not imply any contradiction. It indicates the summit of faith, because it makes no selfish demand, it acknowledges the profound wisdom of the Father, and recognises the existence of a divine pattern of life that includes much more than our individual desires. "Our times are in His hand who saith, A whole I planned . . . trust God, see all, nor be afraid."

The assurance of Jesus is still ours, that all we need for living is given by the Father whose wisdom alone is the arbiter of what is good. That assurance is still offered to all who will put the Kingdom of God first, with all that is implied. We are not to confuse our personal desires with the broader purposes of God, but it has been the happy experience of many to find that their willingness to accept an "either-way" principle resulted in the final removal of adverse inner conditions, bringing them into the great ranges of blessedness. Here they have fitted into the divine pattern, and received the gift of wholeness. Our appeal in prayer is not to a certainty that what we seek is bound to be given, but to a love so understanding that we are willing to leave every issue of life to its perfect way.

Here we come to the place of *affirmation*. We affirm the divine source of the wholeness we seek, the real and present work of God within us or others for whom we intercede, and not least, our thankfulness. We do not wait until we can see or feel the physical healing or mental recovery before giving thanks to God. Faith assures us of far more than we can see or feel! Our first affirmation can be this, *The healing now sought by me comes only from God.*

This should be repeated audibly when alone, though in a quiet and confident tone of voice. There is always an impressiveness produced by our voiced affirmations which goes far into the deep mind. Following this we can repeat the affirmation mentally, then reflect upon its meaning. We shall thus realise the immense power of God. We shall also understand that all other ministries of healing, however scientific and gifted, are forms of divine endowment, though they are never substitutes for the higher work of the Father, which is effective where human skill sometimes proves to be unavailing.

The whole foundation of Christian Healing is in this conviction. There cannot be any doubt of the Source of all things, and in healing, or, to use an even better term, in making whole, we can certainly trace the finger of God through every stage and style of the blessed work. What great reassurances are born as soon as we grasp the fact that God is always seeking to restore His own image in humanity! What sense of consecration comes to us, too, when we understand that He fulfils this divine service in many ways, adapting the fruits of human intelligence to His gracious ends. These "fruits" can be high medical discoveries, more skilful surgical ability, psychological insight, and other beneficial things.

We are living in days when the fulfilment of Christ's Ministry of Healing unto wholeness is manifesting itself in many forms, all of which are to be recognised as coming from God. In His vast plan of redemption God has always brought the knowledge and skills of mankind into the pattern of His purpose, for they have all been of His giving, though some have been perverted into destructive channels, where others have been laid at His feet for constructive service. It is far from contradictory to believe at one and the same time in God alone as the Source of our healing and in the development of medical science, with psychological intuitiveness, as among His appointed channels of healing. Our responsibility is to accord the primacy where it is due, to look above and beyond the channels to their divine Source, and to trust Him for the particular means through which He will give Himself.

The second affirmation can be this, *God's blessed healing power is now at work in perfect activity*, and it should receive the same treatment as the first. By quietly repeating it aloud, as opportunity permits, we are assisted to a firmer acceptance of its truth. Our meditations on it will quickly bring a vivid awareness of its truth. We shall sense and feel an inward cleansing, a quiet process of healing and wholeness, and the lessening of all the accompaniments of sickness such as pain and discomfort. Methodists are traditionally given to singing these great affirmations, for Charles Wesley's hymns are steeped in them, many directly related to both bodily and mental healing, as well as to an assurance of the forgiveness of sins. One of these affirmative couplets perfectly matches our second healing affirmation:

> "And all the attributes divine
> Are now at work for me."

In my pastoral sick visitation I have found a great deal of joyous acceptance when this affirmation has been suggested to the patient. It has no credal or theological pinpricks, nor does it bring the Christian convictions of the patient into conflict at any point. After a time it comes to us, when we continue to affirm this truth, that a ceaseless work of re-creation takes place in every cell of the body, remaking, restoring, renewing, until the perfect standard of wholeness has been reached. We also grow into the realisation that this renewing power is not only taking hold of every bodily infirmity at its cellular source but that it is going still deeper, into the mental origins which have the prior place in physical disharmony. By affirming this conviction we are, spiritually, taken to "the back of beyond", where healing begins, and wholeness exists in spirit, waiting to be manifested outwardly.

I have sometimes witnessed the galvanising effects of the first invitation to sick people to make this affirmation a real and practical part of their healing. By itself it has been responsible for bringing some of them to a new, active interest in Christian Healing as a fact. They have, as if by some startling illumination, entered into a freeing truth and seen that God is not love *by itself*, nor power *by itself*, nor life nor intelligence *by themselves*, but a divine union of them *all*, a union of all the powers that exist, and that these powers are within us, flowing and mingling together with great potency unto the making whole again of what has been broken.

I recall one instance particularly where the patient, a lady of much piety, had been held by the idea that God's will for her was that she should suffer. To say the least, this had made itself a resistance force to the medical attention she rather inconsistently demanded. For some years she lived as an invalid, secretly enjoying herself as such, and finding the sympathies of other people a counteractive to all her doctor's assurances that recovery was possible. When our second affirmation came to her knowledge, the illogical side of her belief about God's will for weakness and sickness was clearly seen. It caused her to ask for conversations about healing as a work of God, and she began to read selected literature about it. She made a full recovery in a short time, and her thinking about God, after that, was in terms of perfect Life.

The third affirmation, also to be treated like the others, can be this, *For the perfect outcome of faith and prayer unto healing, I am thankful to the Father.* When we break this conviction down into its spiritual parts we see the place of thanksgiving in the perfect work of God unto wholeness. Here is the supreme test of our faith, for, if we can be thankful in advance of the blessing, knowing that God's answer to our prayer *will* be given, and that it *must* be the only possible reply, we have reached the highest level of trust. The best credential of our prayer is to feel so confident of the divine grace and goodness that we can offer thanks as a doxology of anticipation.

So far we have seen something of the predisposing convictions and the working affirmations that can bring us into the healing spirit. This Ministry of Healing has the Lord Jesus as its centre and its source, and it leaves no part of our being out of its scope. It is *wholeness* that we seek rather than a limited healing. One of the significant things in the healing ministry of Jesus was the absence of any word from Him that could indicate a limited cure. Nothing that He said before or after His gracious work suggested that a cure had been applied to a part of the person. The instruction was "Be thou made whole".

We certainly believe that the directing force in this work, from our side of it, is expectant, trusting prayer. Whatever else may be ancillary to prayer, such as medical attention in any of its several forms, this is the spearhead of the work. There are channels of healing through which God works other than by direct answers to faith, but it is altogether wrong, in my view, to assume that the Father at any time in history transferred the New Testament and apostolical experience of healing exclusively to science and psychiatry. It is just as wrong to regard prayer and trust as being merely "helpful" in this work, creating a suitable atmosphere for psychosomatic or material remedies. We are sometimes told that there is very great difficulty in ascertaining the order of value where Christian convictions have been combined with medical treatment. For this reason the former is sometimes "played down" as being nothing more than a contributory leaven enabling the materially assisted healing to rise into fullness. May it not be a different and greater factor? I feel sure that many recoveries, whether these have been considered normal to the prognosis, or the surprises that are not infrequent after diagnosis and prognosis, should more properly be accepted as the wholeness given by Christ. This does not cause us to think lightly of medical or "natural" ways. No right-thinking believer in direct Christian Healing would for one moment disparage anything or anybody whose purpose is to bring health and joy to the sick in body or in mind.

Again, nothing in our belief need ever encourage suspicion that we seek to disturb, in any way, the medical, surgical, or psychiatric treatment received by patients who ask for our intercessions. Indeed, the tendency is certainly towards confirming this treatment when it is right. If it is wrong—and it has been known to be so—confident prayer can and does lead to the correct treatment. We must remember that no small part of the Holy Spirit's blessed work is in the direction of checking what is wrong, of correcting mistakes. How else can we regard His enlightening ministry, unless we erroneously limit this to matters of sin, excluding those of sickness? "The mistakes of my life have been many," an old doggerel religious chorus runs. These mistakes are not only moral ones! The work of the Holy Spirit is to get to the root of every wrong, whether this reveals itself in illness or in sin. It reaches the deepest places of the human spirit—"That inmost centre in us all where Truth abides in fullness," as Browning says. By quiet faith in that penetrating power we can obtain the correction of what, otherwise, might never be known, including all errors of judgement or of method, and be led into the effective channels of recovery.

The important thing is to have a well-balanced, ordered approach to Christian Healing. In the truest sense we should be the "friends of all and the enemies of none". No finer brotherhood should exist than within the Fellowship of Healing. As we steadily maintain the end in view, doing the good will of God, becoming fellow-workers together with Him, both our faith and our skill will have a happy partnership. Among intercessors and healing practitioners of all kinds there should be a sacred bond of union. We should be free from ignorant, careless, or prejudiced practice, for the things of God all require the same sane, practical, and exact principle as more temporal responsibilities.

I feel that attention should be drawn to an error we all meet with in our healing service through the Church. There is a curious notion held by some that the larger the number of individuals and intercession groups brought into healing prayer for a sufferer, the more likely it is that recovery will result. By all means let this holy service be shared, but it should be understood that God's healing grace does not await our mass besieging! It is not necessarily the amount of intercession that prevails but its quality. By widening the circle of praying people we do not thereby, of necessity, give evidence of great faith. It may well be the opposite! It may be uncertainty. We can betray doubt of the efficacy of a few, or even of a single intercessor, meeting in Christ's name. It can sometimes mean the evidence of greater faith to restrict the intercessory circle, and not to widen it. The acquiring faith has to be in God Himself, not in the channels. That is why so often the quiet, confident, trusting prayer of the few, as well as that of the patient where possible, has opened the gates of healing, where a widespread scramble for "praying people" may have no discernible effect.

We should remember, too, that the physically felt symptom may mask a spiritual, emotional, or psychological disability. It is now widely believed that many illnesses and mishaps have such an inward origin. This being so, we fail in our expectations of wholeness unless we begin where the trouble began. *In Christian Healing it is often this source that requires our attention rather than the obvious sickness.* The invisible but malignant spiritual, mental, or moral abnormality needs to be treated. This may be sin, or anxiety, or fear, or resentment.

It is always right that we examine ourselves in all honesty to see what the primary cause of our sickness may be—whether we are afraid, or worried, or guilty, for instance. Whatever we may or may not find, we shall certainly bring ourselves to the healing point when we humbly and sincerely open our hearts to God for His perfect cleansing. And then the one thing we should be sure of is our faith in God Himself for His own wisdom, power, and love. The "can and will" elements in His healing are of less moment than our own faith *in the Father as He is in the holiness of His nature.* When we have that, all His work follows and falls into perfect place. Our thought should be given to God as the Centre and Source of every good and gracious thing. There we reach the highest point we can attain both in devotion and in healing. We are to think less of what God does than of who He is. That is the healing height. When we reach it we are in the place where wholeness is possible above the vibrations and potencies that cling to disease and disorder. There we are in the heavenlies where the will of God is always done.

Our prayers should never be of the begging, beseeching kind. When we are ready to receive healing, everything else is ready also. There is never any question of pleading with God as if He needs to be persuaded to graciousness and blessing. The tone of our prayers has to be affirmative and positive. Three elements in such prayer exist: an acknowledgment of the indwelling God as Healer; belief that where He is there is good action; and sincere thankfulness. Strings of prayers are not essential. The simpler we are, the better. The less formal our prayers, the more creative is our consciousness. We should begin at once to act on our prayers by preparing for the normal pursuits of health, rejecting every temptation to "wait and see". We must be wise, of course, acting prudently on our prayer. We should feel our way steadily into the normal again, beginning mentally by refusing every negative thought. "We touch Him in life's throng and press, and we are whole again."

11

THE HEARING EAR AND THE SEEING EYE

by THE REV. DR. J. MICHAEL WILSON

Dr. Wilson, M.B., B.S., M.R.C.S., M.R.C.P., M.D., qualified as a medical practitioner after studying at University College Hospital, London, and joined the staff of Achimota Hospital on the Gold Coast. He then returned to England to prepare for ordination, and served as a curate in a Lancashire parish. Dr. Wilson is now the Chaplain to the Guild of Health, and is the author of The Doctor's Vocation.

"The hearing ear, and the seeing eye, the Lord hath made even both of them" (Prov. 20: 12).

ALL HEALING IS DIVINE

FAMILIARITY BREEDS CONTEMPT! In the grime of a Lancashire industrial parish the family's hands are always grubby. Now I wash my hands and be done with it, but watch the face of my youngster of three alight with joy as he squeezes the soap between his fingers, watching the coloured bubbles with their tiny reflections of the window. Doubtless all explicable in terms of surface tensions and refraction of light, but the *wonder* of it!

The Jews murmured at Jesus because He said, "I am the Bread of Heaven which came down out of heaven. And they said, Is not this Jesus, the son of Joseph, whose father and mother we know? How doth he now say, I am come down out of heaven?" (John 6: 42). A village carpenter's ignorant son—nothing divine about that!

The B.M.A. report on Divine Healing and Co-operation between Doctors and Clergy states: "To summarise, we can find no evidence that there is any type of illness cured by 'Spiritual Healing' alone which could not have been cured by medical treatment which necessarily includes consideration of environmental factors. We find that, whilst patients suffering from psychogenic disorders may be 'cured' by various methods of Spiritual Healing, just as they are by methods of suggestion and other forms of psychological treatment employed by doctors, we can find no evidence that organic diseases are cured solely by such means. The evidence suggests that many cases claimed to be cured are likely to be either instances of wrong diagnosis, remission, or possibly of spontaneous cures." Not much room for the divine! But the facts of a situation are not always the truth of the matter. "Two men looked out from prison bars; the one saw mud and the other saw stars."

No reader of this symposium will be left in any doubt that all healing is God's work. It is His way of re-creating, re-making, restoring a spoilt world: healing not only men's bodies, minds and souls, but also healing the divisions between one party and another, one race and another, one religion and another. "From the Most High cometh healing" (Ecclus. 38: 2). There is nothing more holy or wonderful about healing a patient by prayer than by penicillin, for "the earth is the Lord's and the fullness thereof" (Ps. 24: 1), *but because a thing is understandable, it does not cease to be divine.* The miracles of a hundred years ago are commonplace today. Today's mysteries will be understood tomorrow. There is therefore no frontier between what is scientifically explicable in terms of pathology or physiology, and what is not yet understood by science—a possible field for supernatural healing. Yet this frontier exists in the minds of many writers who speak of "divine intervention" in healing. How can a God who is not only "above all" but also "through all and in all" (Eph. 4: 6), who has made the world and everything in it, be spoken of as "intervening" in it? This is a sub-Christian idea of God. God's Holy Spirit is in every one of us, ceaselessly at work, saving, healing, upholding, expressing Himself. He is there before the doctor is called in. He is there before the child is baptised. Doctor and priest are called to co-operate with that Holy indwelling Spirit. There is no frontier between Him and science: all knowledge is His; without Him there would be no science.

MIRACLES HAPPEN

If by miracles we mean "an act of supernatural power", inexplicable by science, and if our conception of Divine Healing is limited to this field, then as medical research advances, the field of Divine Healing will shrink; but if by miracle we mean "something wonderful", then both G.P. and priest, in their common healing ministry for men and women, can provide us with many examples which cause us to give thanks to God. Our Lord used the word "sign" rather than "miracle" for His acts of healing, and these "signs" *do* happen, both explicable and inexplicable but always wonderful, and the true humility of scientific enquiry and reverence are essential in their study.

Let us examine possible reasons why it continues to be difficult to produce scientifically documented evidence of cases healed by spiritual means:

1. *It is not Possible to Isolate a "Divine Factor".*

In the light of what we have said about the nature of God, how could it be? Jesus Himself used different methods of healing: sometimes a spoken word (John 4: 50), a touch (Matt. 8: 3), spittle (Mark 8: 23), clay followed by washing (John 9: 6); today, doctors, psychiatrists and priests are instruments in God's hands for healing by medicine, analysis or sacrament.

The kind of case for which the miracle-testers are looking is a patient who has come for medical diagnosis, and perhaps had a biopsy which has proved a malignant growth (upon the nature of which there is no dispute, and whose natural history is well known), and who then receives spiritual ministration *and no other treatment*, and who can then be medically followed up regularly for at least five years. One successful case alone might be spontaneous remission (whatever that may mean), so might two or three; but ten or twenty or a hundred, with few failures, would be conclusive.

It would be extremely difficult to fulfil these conditions, but if it *were* possible it would be tempting God. It may look good as a scientific experiment; as a religious one it is puerile. The Mount Carmel type of test is pre-Christian (1 Kings 18), and Jesus rejected putting His miraculous powers to the test in His temptation in the wilderness (Luke 4: 9). It would be wrong to straiten God in His work of making men and women whole to one channel of working. Divine Healing is not a power on tap; it is a power which is always subordinate to love. It is not magic; it is one of the fruits of faith and love.

2. *Medicine is Divorced from Religion.*

The parish priest is the backbone of the Church's Ministry of Healing, just as the G.P. is of the medical profession, but they rarely work together as a unit. A priest who gives one of his sick folk the laying on of hands may only know the diagnosis from what the patient has told him. A "patch of inflammation on the lung", "flu", "an ulcer", "rheumatism"—these are conveniently general terms for a doctor to use pending further investigation, or the results of therapy. But they are valueless as evidence upon which to make a claim of Divine Healing.

Nor has a priest access to X-rays, or biopsies except in rare cases, supposing he did wish to make further enquiries. And when one of his people, just back from the infirmary, says, "Father, it's T.B., could I be anointed?", the priest does not at once ask, "Did they diagnose it by X-ray *and* sputum *and* guinea pig?"—he lifts up his heart in thanksgiving and gets on with the job, and both priest and patient then face the spell in the sanatorium without concern. But just sometimes that visit to the sanatorium becomes unnecessary: it is then that one man goes down on his knees, while another thinks that they must have got the X-ray plates muddled.

3. *Patients Dislike an Atmosphere of Unbelief.*

Patients who have been spiritually healed naturally dislike being exposed to investigations which throw doubt upon their healing. A person spiritually healed has already turned his back upon the past and is looking to the future in hope and with thanksgiving: his attitude may well be—"What's the use of raking *that* over now?" A long series of investigations and follow-ups may be just the thing to upset the patient's faith, sow seeds of doubt, and cause a relapse. It all depends on the way it is done, upon the personalities of the investigators and the patients, and the purpose of their joint enquiry.

THE DESIRE FOR PROOF

What are we trying to prove? That God *can* heal organic disease? That God *does* heal organic disease? Or are we trying to understand something more of the way in which God is working His purposes out in the world, with special reference to bodily disease? Who wants to know? The believer or the unbeliever? The believer is always concerned to know more about God, so that he may co-operate more fully with His will. It is nearly fifty years ago that one of the first attempts was made to bring doctors and priests together; and the statement following that conference held in 1910 suggested a careful enquiry into the evidence for cases of Spiritual Healing. And now the Archbishop's Commission on Divine Healing and Co-operation between Doctors and Clergy has been seeking evidence, and the British Medical Association have published the results of their enquiry on behalf of the Commission.

The medical profession, too, is concerned to establish the truth of claims widely made by faith healers, spiritual healers and healers with charismatic gifts. Healing is a happy hunting ground for every type of crank from the frankly pagan dabbler in magic to those who use God's name but serve not His cause. Both Medicine and the Church are concerned with truth, but an over-concern with *results* may blind us from seeing *Him who is the Truth*.

Is all this incidental, then? The disciple of Jesus Christ is sent to preach the Kingdom of God, to heal the sick, and to baptise all nations. "Seek ye first His Kingdom and His righteousness; and all these things shall be added unto you" (Matt. 6: 33). Health is not therefore an end in itself, but an asset to be used in the service of God's Kingdom. Edward Wilson of the Antarctic, a man who spent himself for others, wrote in a letter: "I can't bear people who always take for granted that one's main object is to save up one's health and strength, eyesight and what not, for when one is sixty. How on earth can they tell whether one is going to reach thirty? I think it's better to wear a thing while it's good and new, patching the odd corners as they wear out, instead of putting it away carefully year after year till at last the moths get in, and you find it's no good when at last you think you will wear it."

The very core of Jesus' message is the spread of the Kingdom of God by word (preaching to the people) and by deed (healing the sick, death and resurrection), and the healing of the sick was not just a tactical bolster to the faith of the early Church but a visible proof of the power of the Spirit over the physical. And Jesus revealed the nature of our loving Father just as surely by acts of healing as by His words: for His word was with power (Luke 4: 36). And just as surely today can we judge the presence or absence of the Kingdom of God and the power of the Resurrection Life by the presence or the absence of an effective healing ministry in the Church. Making men whole is one of the touchstones of divine action among men.

Nor must we be tempted to look only for spiritual healing and not also for bodily healing. *It is absolutely true that spiritual healing is directed first to the inner disharmony which inhibits the true functioning of the spirit within a man,* and so releases the power of the spirit and enables it to perform its true function of expressing itself in healing and perfection. That inner healing must also be seen to be expressed throughout a person's whole nature, soul and mind and body. For that is the meaning of the Incarnation, that spirit expresses itself through matter. Jesus made men whole, and the Bible uses the same word for both "saving" and "making whole". Therefore acts of healing are *not* merely incidental to the main Christian task of preaching the Gospel and baptising all nations—"Blessed are the eyes which see the things that ye see" (Luke 10: 23). But they *are* incidental in the sense that work for the Kingdom comes *first*, and power is subordinate to love.

In a case of peptic ulcer due to worry in a God-less patient many agencies will contribute to healing: rest in bed, diet, drip feeding, and efforts by the chaplain, psychiatrist or welfare officer to clear up the worries. Healing may be purely physical, followed by a relapse, if the deep causes are not dealt with. But the Church's Ministry of Healing seeks to make the patient whole, which means bringing patients to know and love our Lord, and to give their lives to Him for better or for worse, and this "conversion" is the beginning of wholeness. *There are therefore spiritual as well as material facts to be ascertained in the investigation of the results of Divine Healing.*

Spiritual Authenticity in a Case of Divine Healing

The healing of organic disease—such as pneumonia, appendicitis, malaria—is an everyday occurrence in hospitals; such healing is by natural means, medicine and surgery. Often enough the patient goes home none the wiser; God *seems* hardly to have entered into the matter. Much of the work of "healers" is at this level, and therefore competes with medicine as a means of relief, but in a person who has been spiritually healed the whole person is changed, and there are certain features which give the healing a spiritual authenticity which a fellow believer will instantly appreciate.

(*a*) *There is a loss of self-concern.* The person puts God at the centre of his life, and so enters into his right relationship with his Heavenly Father. Always a child of God, he now claims his sonship and prays, "Father". This loss of self-concern is often evident, too, in his attitude to the disease. The patient may so give himself into the hands of God that his attitude is now one of complete trust, for healing or not for healing, for life or for death.

(*b*) *There is a reverent reserve about healing.* This is something precious that has happened, and he will not go about boasting, but will willingly use his experience for the encouragement of others but not as a public spectacle.

(*c*) *There is new life.* Not only is there this new Godward relationship, but there is a new relationship with his fellow men. Not only does he learn to pray "Father", but also to pray "Our Father": there is a new social re-orientation. This crippled case of polio is now an active worker for the Church and has founded several groups of people to pray for the sick. This case of malignant growth has now dedicated his life to helping others who suffer from that from which he was saved. This woman has been saved for her husband and her children, and how she slaves for them! When we come to God for healing we never know what we are going to get, for we must learn to drop our requests and come to Him for WHAT HE IS, and not for what we want, or what He gives. We give ourselves to Him for His good purposes, not ours, and the result may turn our lives upside-down.

Now unselfishness, humility and religious conversion are not facts which science can easily assess, but they are facts which one human being can recognise in another. They are perfectly valid evidence of a spiritual change, and they have a relevance not only to life in this world but to life hereafter, because this new life *is* the life of the hereafter being lived in the here and now, and it is in this respect that Spiritual Healing differs from natural healing—in its meaning for eternity.

"We must resist the temptation to elevate the healing of the body to the prime place in our thoughts or works. After all, the removal of a cancer by surgery is only one event in a life that is eternal, and the importance of the operation must be judged against the background of eternity. Perhaps it brings the patient for the first time to face up to his relationship to God, in which case the operation, which gave the patient a scant three months' further life and provided a blot in the surgeon's survival records, was from God's point of view a success. Perhaps the operation which gave the patient a further thirty years in which to tyrannise his unfortunate family, and provided the surgeon with an excellent 'show case' for his students, was from God's point of view a failure, because it merely confirmed the patient in his desperately selfish attachment to himself and his own pleasures. Healing cannot be regarded as complete unless it results from or leads to a deeper committed discipleship."[1]

SEEKING SIGNS

We have thought about that deeper committed discipleship—new life—which is the beginning of Wholeness, but what about the power of visible healings to attract men to Jesus? In the temptations in the wilderness Jesus rejected the temptation to do something spectacular in order to win men. Entry into the Kingdom is the free response of heart and will to the love of God: it can never be forced, and the attempt to produce spectacular public healings in our day, in the present climate of scientific belief, or to produce a nicely attested series of cases proving the power of Divine Healing, will either defeat its own purpose or lead men into the wrong Kingdom. God does not work like that, and Jesus rejected the desire of the Pharisees for a sign, because God's power is always subordinate to His

[1] J. M. Wilson, *The Doctor's Vocation* (Guild of Health Pamphlet, 1957), p 5.

love. He will love us, and He will have us love Him, but cupboard love and rape are not the same as love freely given and received.

"Let him now come down from the cross and we will believe on Him" (Matt. 27: 42): thus the world desires its *sign* first, but Jesus teaches quite consistently by word and deed that *faith* must come first and then signs will follow. He said, "All things whatsoever ye pray and ask for, believe that ye have received them and ye shall have them" (Mark 11: 24); and to Thomas He said, "Because thou hast seen me thou hast believed; blessed are they that have not seen, and yet have believed" (John 20: 29). Imagine, too, the ten lepers on their way to show themselves to the priests; they had only to look down at their hands to see that they were still leprous—but they believed and obeyed, and *as they went* they were cleansed (Luke 17: 14).

So today, after Holy Unction, "the patient should feel that he has been given inward liberation from the power of sin and that the disharmony in the soul, which is the real disease and cause of his physical sickness, has been healed. His prayer life should now be directed to thanksgiving for healing and to quiet and expectant confidence in God's power and love working within for his wholeness. There should be no anxious enquiries as to his condition and no talk about his symptoms. Faith believes first and sees afterwards; and it is this joyful expectant confidence in God's love and power working within which enables Him to do His work of healing."[2]

It is also the method of science to think out and make a theory and then put it to the test; belief first, then proof by using it. The way of the world is "Let's see first", but Jesus provided a way to a deeper faith which can help to a reversal of this way of life: "Believe me for the very works' sake" (John 14: 11). Dr. Temple refers to this as a second-best recognition of Jesus, but it may grow.[3]

[2] Jim Wilson, *Redemption of the Common Life* (Dobson, 1950), p. 160.
[3] *Readings in St. John's Gospel*: comment on John 14: 11.

THE COST

We see Jesus' works of healing as an integral part of His good news of the Kingdom, an essential part of His revelation of the nature of His Father; so today healing is an integral part of the Church's mission to the world, an essential part of her teaching to men and women about a God of love, and a Saviour who has died and risen and lives in His Church, strong to save and to make whole. Because works of healing are primarily the *result* of faith and not demonstrations of power to inspire faith, they will appear as the fruits of an obedient ministry by a faithful Church.

We know that Jesus mentioned faith (Matt. 17: 20) and prayer (Mark 9: 29) as necessary for healing work, and obedience to the Father's will is evident in His own life. These things are demanded of a faithful Church, and the Ministry of Healing is a corporate gift to the Church, just as sickness and suffering are also corporate, not individual. So it is as a representative of the Church that the priest footslogs his parish to bring comfort to the dying, cheer to the widow, healing and patience to the sick, forgiveness to the penitent, and the overflowing, generous love of God with equal charity to the good and the bad.

Cheap grace is the hearty desire of every man today, and in the realm of Spiritual Healing there are many wolves in sheep's clothing offering ease and comfort. Artificial pearls may be attractive, even valuable, but what a tragic substitute for the pearl of great price! Grace is never cheap, and discipleship is costly, for the sign of the Christian religion is the Cross, not a feather bed. Faith, prayer and obedience to the will of the Father are the activities in the life of the Church which will strengthen her in her mission to preach the Kingdom and to heal.

THE CONDITIONS

It remains to consider the kind of conditions under which supernatural healing could be investigated scientifically for the revelation of further truth about God and His good purposes for us. The healing of organic disease by spiritual means and its investigation requires a Christian environment, and will occur incidentally to the work of spreading the Kingdom of God. A group of hospital chaplains, working with the full status of members of the hospital staff, with the confidence of their medical colleagues, and access to the clinical notes on which to make their own entries, might after twenty years or so be able to produce some very interesting material for study.

Ideally, it seems to me, we need a Christian Mission Hospital staffed by a team of Christian doctors, nurses and ministers of all denominations, which could investigate the effectiveness of different means of healing, such as laying on of hands, unction, prayer, and perhaps gain new insight into those powers which God pours through men for the blessing of men. This would enable such work to be done as part of our service to the Kingdom in loving and reverent enquiry.

Familiarity breeds contempt, but not for the lover of Christ. A loaf of bread, a cup of cold water, a lily growing in a field, a sparrow falling to the ground, are all full of deep meaning, for they help to bridge the gap between the world of feelings and the world of spirit, lifting our hearts to God. The G.P. injecting polio vaccine, the priest laying his hands upon a head, the nurse taking temperatures, the psychiatrist patiently questing, and the theatre team at full stretch, are all, whether they know it or not, living in two worlds, the world of the senses and the world of the spirit. God is using them all, and they have only to lift up their hearts to Him in wonder and love, to pass from earth to heaven, and bring the power of heaven to earth.

★ Outstanding Books ★